Y0-DBL-098

The Expert From Out of Town

Marketing a Business Nationwide

Anthony F. Perry
Corporate Trainer and Speaker

Edited by Mike Sion
Illustrated by Brian Crane

Nationwide Marketing • Reno, Nevada

© 1996 by Anthony Perry, Nationwide Marketing

For information about permission to reproduce
selections from this book, write to:

Permissions, Nationwide Marketing
P.O. Box 12814
Reno, Nevada 89510

All rights reserved. No part of this book may be reproduced or transmitted in
any form or by any means, electronic or mechanical, including
photocopying, recording, the internet, or by any information storage or
retrieval system, without written permission from Nationwide Marketing,
except for the inclusion of quotations in a review.

The Expert from Out of Town is a registered trademark of Nationwide
Marketing Consultants Reno, Nevada.

Although the author has exhaustively researched all sources to ensure the
accuracy and completeness of the information contained in this book, we
assume no responsibility for errors, inaccuracies, omissions, or any
inconsistency herein. Any slights of people or organizations are
unintentional. Readers should use their own judgment and/or consult
financial experts for specific application to their individual situations.

Edited by Mike Sion
Cover and inside cartoons by Brian Crane
Grammar and sentence / paragraph structure checked by Lana Hedlind
Cover graphic design by Mark Mckinnon

Contact Information for Anthony Perry:
Nationwide Marketing
P.O. Box 12814
Reno, NV 89510

Library of Congress Catalog Card Number: 97-92201

ISBN# 0-9652694-1-8

97 98 99 00 / 10 9 8 7 6 5 4 3 2 1
Printed in the United States of America

To Mom

Table of Contents

INTRODUCTION

My name is Tony Perry, the expert from out of town. It has a nice ring to it, does it not? *The expert from out of town.* The phrase conjures up visions of the ultra-professional: the assertive, absolute authority in his or her field, the person who commands so much business he or she is ultimately selective in accounts taken on. Many people may be shocked to learn that there is really only one fundamental difference separating this special species from the mass of business persons: The expert from out of town is simply an entrepreneur who capitalizes on a national market versus a local market. In this book I will explain to you how to become a member of this select breed.

Most of us have probably witnessed the phenomenon of a local business, firm, or government agency calling someone from out of town to advertise for a campaign, contract for a new building, or consult on a study. Nine times out of ten, there are 50 people in town who can handle the account just as well. Hiring the out-of-towner is more than just a fad or trend. More often than not, it is the norm. The really lucrative jobs do not go to the local guy, but to the expert from out of town. The point of this book is: why fight it? You should become the expert from out town!

THE ADVANTAGES OF BECOMING the expert from out of town are apparent from the start. As the expert, you need no longer worry about vying for business with everyone on your block. Instead, you'll be selling your services in the out-of-town market, which is very likely several hundred, even several thousand times larger! There is also a subtle edge that comes from the mystique, if you will, of being the expert from out of town. It is connected with that old adage: *familiarity breeds contempt* .

Consider the insurance agent who pounds the pavement to sell automobile, life, and homeowner's insurance. The agent goes to Chamber of Commerce functions, networks through friends and relatives, and diligently utilizes local mailing and telephone lists. Unfortunately, the pour soul is competing with a large pack of agents in town doing exactly the same thing. His face is merely one in the crowd.

This can be true in whatever one's field may be: advertising, architecture, political consulting, construction, legal representation, insurance, et cetera. The expert from out of town, this entity from the great unknown, is perceived as a superior being. In fact, people not only perceive this — they believe it! It is amazing: people believe that if they are hiring someone from out of town, they are getting an expert. This is exactly what I'm going to teach you to be: the expert from out of town.

Among the things you will learn are:

• How to analyze your field to find your **niche**.
• How to create a **façade**, including demanding to be paid cash on delivery (C.O.D.) — not because you need the money, but because YOU'RE AN EXPERT!
• How to use **marketing** and **advertising** techniques that work.
• How to establish your **first clients**.
• How to avoid **Pitfalls** in the national market (such as kickbacks).

In sum, I'll be sharing with you the lessons I learned the hard way along the road to becoming an expert from out of town.

THIS BOOK SPRINGS FROM my own experience in becoming the expert from out of town. My trades are graphic design and printing. My niche is the international touring sector of the entertainment industry. To put it in plain English, my small corporation in Reno, Nevada produces backstage concert security passes and other graphics and printing for the biggest names in the music industry, including Whitney Houston, U2 and the Rolling Stones. My business also handles security credentials for such clients as the San Francisco 49ers and the United Nations.

I began ten years ago by founding an entertainment division for a printing company I worked for. Over four years ago, I left to start my own company. Today, the company I'm president of, PERRi Entertainment Services Inc., grosses in excess of $1 million a year. It is characteristic of the business world that there are at least a dozen other businesses in Reno that could have positioned themselves in this international market, yet I was the one who accomplished it!

When representatives from Carnegie Hall and Radio City Music Hall began coming to me, it dawned upon me: I was an expert from out of town. It was at that moment I stopped trying to drum up local business. Now my market base is two hundred and fifty million.

It can work this way for you, too. I firmly believe that there are hundreds of fields that can be exploited by experts from out of town. In Chapter 12, I will randomly run through a telephone book to point out a number of them. When you have absorbed the lessons of this book, you, too, will have all the tools necessary to become the expert from out of town!

CHAPTER ONE
"My First Out of Town Account"

Glenn is a local contractor. He's from Reno, my home town. I mention him because there are a lot of people out there who stumble upon the prospect of becoming the expert from out of town, but they don't carry through by focusing their energy correctly. They qualify as experts, yet don't even realize it! Glenn, however, is one of the lucky ones. He spent the early part of his career working for a general contractor. A small army of contractors in big white pickups can be seen cruising the city's streets on a regular basis. Reno is said to have the most pickup trucks per capita in the world.

Now, if you live in a town of about 200,000 people, like Glenn, and you want to get 200 clients (one percent of the market) it's a hard row to hoe, but Glenn used his head. Over a matter of years, through a construction company he worked for, he gained an expertise in building jails. Soon, he found himself to be a specialist in supervising jail construction. He found his niche.

Of course, even with skyrocketing crime, there are only a limited number of jails that can be built in one area. Glenn realized this so he marketed his specialty all across the country and gained steady, lucrative employment with companies who bid on jail projects. This is the way it turned out. Glenn's list of job offers kept getting longer.

This concept applies to just about anyone, from plumbing to printing to graphics to consulting. The possibilities are absolutely endless for becoming an expert in a particular field. You just have to find your niche, as Glenn did.

TO TELL THE TRUTH, I didn't consciously set out to become the expert from out of town in the printing trade. There was no book such as this available to me in book stores. Like most people, I had no notion such a marketing strategy even existed. My knowledge was of graphics and printing, specifically posters, fliers, backstage security passes, and credentials. As with most decent-sized cities, Reno seemed full of opportunity. There were local special events, shows, and concerts. However, as every small-business entrepreneur discovers at the start: breaking in ain't easy. The first few months for me were very discouraging.

When I began canvassing for customers, I was very young (21 to be exact). I had a beard and long hair, with no large office or tall building to help my appearance; rather, I was working out of a confined space my employer graciously granted me. In short, gaining that immediate customer respect on a handshake seemed impossible for me.

The first accounts one goes after in my business are concerts, state fairs, and other special events. I approached proprietors and promoters, but they didn't give me the time of day. To them, I was just a local nobody. They would only "deal with the big boys." In fact, that was a line I heard early on. It impacted me so much, I'll remember it until the day I die.

Enthusiastically, I had gone to see the owner of a local entertainment sound and lighting company. His outfit had a small studio downstairs where local and regional acts recorded cassettes and CD's. I had the vague notion of producing album covers, posters, and perhaps even passes and tickets for shows. The man told me, "I'm sorry, we deal with the big boys here." I left his office with head bowed, thinking, "Man, this guy just doesn't want to deal with me."

This, by the way, is how business inferiority complexes start. Little did I know that the rejection from the sound and lighting company was the boost I needed. Far from throwing in the towel, I doubled my determination to make it as a graphic designer and printer for the touring industry. Thank heaven, I realized I was burning myself out trying to get that first customer from the local market.

Out of necessity, I began to hunt for business out of town. I sent mailers to potential clients around the country, trying to get sample packets of my work in the hands of decision makers. I wish I could say that fate stepped in at this point, but it didn't. By the end of six months, I still had zip to show for all my efforts. I had just about given up when I heard Billy Joel had a concert scheduled at Lawlor Events Center, Reno's chief arena. The day of the show, as roadies toiled to assemble the stage and sound equipment, I made my way up to Lawlor Events Center. I'd learned through concert trade publications that Joel's production manager was named Bobby Thrasher. I handed my package of sample products, addressed to Thrasher, to a security guard at the front gate. Then I went to lunch.

When I returned to work, several phone messages awaited me. They were from Mr. Thrasher. With my heart pounding, I went back to Lawlor and introduced myself. Little did I know that my image with him was superior to my image in my own community. All he knew was that I was an expert in producing graphics and printing. He had no idea I was the bright-eyed young guy who'd been immediately dismissed by the local sound and lighting company.

That day, Bobby Thrasher was having trouble with the company that had been making the backstage passes for Billy Joel. He now needed someone to fill in for the rest of the tour, including producing the passes for Joel's upcoming concert in Moscow. It was going to be a landmark event. This occurred in the mid 1980s; the Iron Curtain had yet to fall. I designed the credentials Joel needed and had my first customer!

Looking back years later, I understand what Bobby

Thrasher must have thought. If a business representative has enough confidence to call an out-of-town person, his outfit must be very good. To my delight, I found that being the expert from out of town meant being placed on a pedestal. You'll find out the same thing.

AFTER HAVING HAD THE OPPORTUNITY to serve my first customer, I recognized that to lure Billy Joel, David Bowie, and other similar big accounts, I needed to position myself as the expert from out of town.

All of a sudden, business started coming in. I wanted to pinch myself. In fact, it took a year before I came to accept that my clients were not being duped by looking upon me as an expert. After all, I was an expert. I was successfully producing graphics and printing on a regular basis for the biggest concert draws in the world. At the same time, I didn't let myself forget that there were other printers in Reno, and in every town, who had the ability to handle the accounts I was getting. What was holding them back from achieving the same success? Themselves.

I've now spent over ten years working with clients from out of town. I've reached the point where I am able to share my accumulated knowledge. I know about becoming, and being, the expert from out of town. I know the tricks. My right to write this book comes from having experienced the ups and downs. I have changed corporations, been out of a job, and repositioned myself in the national market. I've learned by doing. I don't have a business degree, or even a college degree, but I do have a Ph.D. in the Real World.

I DON'T WRITE BOOKS for a living. This is my first such project, but if there's anything I know about, it's marketing a specialized business nationwide. I also know there isn't any other kind of book like this. It is not about starting a home-based business; it is not about starting a mass-mailing business. This is a book about becoming an expert in an area, finding your niche, and focusing your energy on a national market.

An enormous number of how-to-succeed titles fill bookstore shelves. I've read most of them. All too often, I turn the last pages only to wonder whether I've learned anything at all. Far too many seem to be nothing more than motivational books. They don't offer the fine details on how to run a business. This book strives to be completely different. By the time you've finished it, you should have absorbed the necessary information to succeed exactly as I have succeeded. As you make your way forward on this rewarding business journey, I know this book will serve as a valuable reference guide.

There is one more thing I want to say at this point. My motivation to write this book comes from a burning desire to share my experience with those who have entrepreneurial spirits and the guts to pursue and persevere at becoming the expert from out of town. This book could begin one of the biggest revolutions for entrepreneurs in every small town in America. My fondest hope is that it will serve as a manifesto for every big dreamer in small towns across the country. It will give them the confidence to go after the biggest accounts, and not only compete with, but actually possess the edge over rivals in the big cities.

Over and over I've heard the refrain (and surely, you have too) that goes something like this: "I've got to get out of this small place; it's holding me back!" People with this attitude yearn to move out, they think moving out means moving up. Every time I hear about entrepreneurs who wants to get out and move to the Big City, I want to tell them that they have no clue what asset they're sitting on! That's why I believe in this book so much. It is absolutely phenomenal how much more respect one receives as the expert from out of town, compared to just another fish in the pond — whether the "pond" be the puddle of a small town or the sea of a metropolis. I could shift our printing business to Lakeview, Oregon, and have the exact same clients, the Billy Joels, the Michael Jacksons, and the Rolling Stones. They're out there for you, too.

Ironically, despite PERRi Inc.'s impressive list of clients, the local clique in Reno still looks upon me as the little guy sitting over in an industrial area of town, trying to get their business "the guy who isn't dialed in to the local business scene". We still can't land printing accounts with the Reno Rodeo or Nevada State Fair. Yet, PERRi Entertainment is handling some of the largest state fairs and rodeo finals around the country!

That's why I'm hell-bent on my theory of the expert from out of town. It worked for me, and it can work for you. Ultimately, this book is meant to change not only the way you do business, but the way you think of yourself in the grander scheme of things. Realize that business isn't as hard as you think it is. There is an incredible comfort zone in finding out how much business is really out there. As long as you put hard work into absorbing this book, you will be on your way to becoming the expert from out of town.

Glenn, whom I mentioned at the beginning of this chapter, could have spent all his years working for one construction company, but he found his niche in the national market building jails. Now, in that specialized area, Glenn is the expert from out of town.

Two chapters from now, we'll examine how to prepare to take the plunge. But first, we'll look a little more closely at why customers are psychologically drawn to the expert from out of town.

CHAPTER TWO
"Why? The Sociological Phenomenon"

Bestowing automatic respect upon the stranger is as old as human nature. Unfortunately, taking the native for granted is, too. The stranger carries no visible baggage; therefore, he has mystique. This is not so of the neighbor, family member, or friend whose foibles, faults, and vices are known to all. "Familiarity breeds contempt," as the saying goes.

Consider the carpenter who lived in a small farming town a number of centuries ago. His skills eventually went beyond working with wood to healing the sick and working miracles. Was his home town impressed? "He is no better than we are, he is just a carpenter, Mary's boy," a fellow resident of the town said. Thus runs the account in the New Testament (Mark 6:4).

The carpenter, whose name, of course, was Jesus, had an explanation for the scorn he received in Nazareth: "A prophet is honored everywhere except his own country, and among his own people." The biblical passage (Matthew 13:57) continues: "And so he did only a few great miracles there, because of their disbelief." But as the carpenter's reputation swelled, even Nazareth was swayed. As it says in John 4:44, "the Galileans would welcome him with open arms, for he had been in Jerusalem at the Passover celebration and they had seen some of his miracles."

In other words, Jesus first had to go to Jerusalem, the big city, to build his reputation as a man of God and great teacher before his own townsfolk would appreciate him. This raises the question, if the founder of one of the world's great religions had a tough time winning over the local crowd, do you think your path will be any easier? Often, the hardest people to impress are your own neighbors, peers, family, and friends. They "knew you when." The moral: Your roots can strangle you.

HISTORY IS RIFE WITH exemplars of author Thomas Wolfe's dictum, "You can't go home again."

The Italian painter, sculptor, architect, inventor, engineer, scientist, and philosopher Leonardo da Vinci, arguably the most prodigious intellect the human race has produced, avoided his childhood town of Anchiano. Once, in his far-ranging endeavors, Leonardo penned a theoretical passage on the formation of rivers. He listed Anchiano on the map, then struck it out. Shall we leave it only to the historians to ponder why? Could it have been a deep-seated need in Leonardo to not diminish his own aura by acknowledging that even a colossal genius such as himself was once a dependent child?

There once was a talented guitarist who left his sleepy, rainy city and entered the Army. After he hurt his back in a paratrooping jump, he was discharged. Soon, he found himself playing backup for touring rock 'n' roll and blues performers. He displayed not only an uncommon virtuosity on the fretboards, but a unique flair for the theatrical. The outrageous Little Richard refused to have stage hands shine a spotlight on this young phenomenon. He found the crowd exploded with delight as the guitarist played the strings with his teeth, upstaging Mr. "Tutti Frutti." In time, fate intervened. A manager brought the guitarist over to England and found him a band. Jimi Hendrix was finally afforded the star status that had escaped him in his own country. In his home town, he'd been just another poor kid who'd dropped out of high school.

Local Boy

At the height of stardom, Hendrix returned to his alma mater to speak at a student assembly. He froze, stammered and after a few questions, left the stage. Two years later, he passed away. The reward of his untimely death? His stature grew to mythological proportions. His grave outside Seattle became a shrine.

IT IS A PHENOMENON, THIS STRUGGLING for recognition and respect in your own back yard when a more receptive climate awaits you somewhere else. It is almost always easier to command respect from a faceless stranger on a long-distance business call than it is from a local who knows you.

I have had very few experiences in my career where I've gotten to meet or have dinner with clients, and actually bonded as friends. Our conversations are normally very short and to the point. That's not to say the calls are impersonal. We have chatted about families and so on, but neither side has time to really get to know the other. Scant private information is shared. This is a good thing.

Once people get a little bit of an edge on you, find out your baggage, quirks, career stumbles, busted relationships, and physical ailments, your façade is ripped away, and they've seen the emperor without his clothes. In fact, I'd like you to try out a little exercise as your business builds. Make notes about the people you're doing business with on a regular basis. Analyze how much they really know about you. You might be surprised to discover that those who are easiest to work with, and whom you're making the most money from, may know the least about your private life.

I probably have more difficulties with clients who have been with me for years than I do with newer customers. To the long-termers I've become familiar, and thus they hit me up more often for favors and pressure me into quick turnarounds.

Out of Town Expert™

THERE ARE TWO MAIN points in this chapter. We have just discussed the first, that you must first free yourself from the bondage of familiarity. People love to find fault with others; your own community knows you too well to be impressed. It is human nature. The second point is also bound up in human nature. It is that you need to take advantage of a quality I term, "artificial superiority."

Consider that the largest industry in the world is the travel industry. People are drawn to the strange and the exotic. They would rather fly 3,000 miles to experience foreigners speaking a strange tongue in a small mountain village than drive 150 miles to some hick town in the boonies in their very own state. Inborn in our species is the drive to explore, to seek out the new.

Why are the latest women's fashions from Paris or Milan so intoxicating, as opposed to those from the United States? Conversely, why is everything American, from pop music to fast food to T-shirts and jeans, all the rage among the youth of Europe? Because "over there" is better.

"Artificial superiority" is the term I've coined to describe the quality we bestow upon things beyond our domain. The attraction to artificial superiority is one main reason why a buyer will seek out a business from out-of-town instead of a local shop to fill his or her needs.

The owner of the local entertainment sound and lighting company who shot me down with, "We deal with the big boys here," did not have the intent of nipping some local kid's enterprise in the bud. Rather, he brushed me off because he was looking to grow, to build new contacts with out-of-town suppliers, to break out of his comfort zone and network in his industry. This was also because he was convinced that out-of-town businesses were better, artificial superiority.

When you've become a specialist in your niche, marketing yourself out of town, you will be capitalizing on the "artificial superiority" factor.

IN SUM, MERELY BY positioning yourself in the nationwide marketplace, you'll have three strong factors working for you, giving you energy.

• You will have escaped whatever perceptions of shortcomings you have been saddled with in your own town.

• You will possess the aura of artificial superiority automatically because you're from out of town.

• You will enjoy the elevated status of the specialist.

Incidentally, you might also net an unexpected dividend. Once you've achieved significant success as the expert from out of town, you may find that those in your own community suddenly view you in a completely new light. When it happens, relish it. Just remember to try not to be too much of a snob toward those who snubbed you in the past.

CHAPTER THREE
"Taking the Plunge, and Knowing Where"

So many people are working in jobs they don't like. Most of us have worked for other people — someone else's business — and we've heard the tired exchanges of co-workers.

"How're ya doin'?"

"Overworked and underpaid!"

Or: "Hangin' in there, it's Friday!"

Most people do the best they can, recognizing that if they work a little harder, they'll get a little further. But too many people end up putting in their time, anxious to leave when 5 o'clock rolls around. Few ever go that extra mile to get ahead, reasoning, however wisely or unwisely, that the extra effort will either go unnoticed, unappreciated, or merely serve to accrue the boss's good fortune, not their own.

There are also those who talk a good game about "going out on my own." They have dreams, perhaps even written plans, about starting a small business or becoming a consultant, but only a slim percentage ever follow through. The great question is: "What does it take to be a risk-taker?" I could toss out platitudes such as, "You've got to be brave," or, "You've got to stand tall," but that's not what it takes.

What it takes is motivation to do something that you know is going to work, and that you're going to enjoy working on. Perhaps this sounds simple, but if we break it up into its parts, we'll see how others have failed.

No one is going to succeed in a business without the utter conviction that one's business idea is solid, nor is anyone going to carry through on the hard work of researching, building, and sustaining an entrepreneurial enterprise without love for doing the work.

EVERYONE WHO HAS ELECTED to take a risk at any time in his or her life has done so by savoring the challenge at hand. You don't endure the strenuous toil of mountain-climbing and its inherent dangers unless you relish the work. If you're not going to enjoy the struggle ahead, the process that any risk-taking involves, you're not going to succeed.

Consider a man who hates his job: he saves $20,000 and intends to take that once-in-a-lifetime shot at starting a business. He buys an entrepreneur's magazine, reads about "hot" new businesses, then goes out and buys a franchise in a field he doesn't know and doesn't love. Let's say the gentleman gets sold on buying a coffee shop (Espresso is really big right now!) and invests his life savings. He persuades his friends and family to ante up as well. All eyes are fixed on dollar signs.

What happens? The man fails because he doesn't love what he's doing. He hasn't analyzed the details. He has no burning desire to learn all about the latest coffee blends and flavorings. He isn't motivated to spend hours mastering the espresso machine. He can't even relate to the clientele. He has no idea that young people with pierced nostrils and eyebrows, whose clothes carry the stench of clove cigarettes go along with owning a coffeehouse.

You have to live and breathe what you're going to do in order to succeed at it. You have to love your work. You will reach the top of the mountain because you crave the climb.

THE QUESTION THEN ARISES of how to choose what business is right for you. You may believe you have already found the right business. Nevertheless, I recommend that you read this chapter. It may help you ascertain whether it really is right for you, and whether or not your field is too broad.

Choosing the correct business is, obviously, the most important step any would-be entrepreneur can undertake. What is the right choice for you? The answer is derived from this equation: **KNOWLEDGE + PASSION = THE BUSINESS FOR YOU TO MASTER**. Or, to state it another way: **OCCUPATION + HOBBY = THE BUSINESS FOR YOU TO MASTER**.

This is precisely what happened when I entered the field of graphic design and printing for the international touring industry. In short, I took my knowledge of printing (gleaned from working for a printing company for five years) and coupled it with my love of entertainment production (cultivated in high school via my passion for community theater).

Printing (**KNOWLEDGE**) + theater/entertainment (**PASSION**) = graphic design and printing for the entertainment industry (**THE BUSINESS FOR ME TO MASTER**).

Let's consider three hypothetical scenarios of how this equation can play itself out.

Scenario No. 1: Remember Glenn the contractor from chapter one? Glenn works hard. He's good at what he does and he makes a good living, but he's not content working as a supervisor for a construction company. He wants to be his own man.

As a boy, Glenn, like many others, wanted to be a policeman. But, as Glenn grew up, he never got the opportunity. He was drafted, went to war and returned, needing a job right away. He ended up in construction, learning a trade.

Now Glenn's old interest in law enforcement isn't entirely extinguished. He devours detective novels, loves court television programs, and he's worn out his video of Shawshank Redemption. He even has a pipe dream about going to law school at night.

It so happens that the construction company begins winning bids on jail projects. Glenn proves himself not only highly enthusiastic to tackle these projects as a supervisor, but he quickly becomes an expert on jail-building. In fact, his interest leads him to delve into the background of famous prisons, their construction, and even their histories. Eventually, he is able to leave his employer and market himself as a special project manager for hire to companies building correctional facilities.

Scenario No. 2: Lorrie, an entertainment industry minion, gets burned out on the behind-the-scenes drudgery of organizing and producing concerts. She loves rock 'n' roll; she just tires of the stress of day-to-day touring. She ends up, almost by chance, as a travel agent "between careers."

To her surprise, Lorrie discovers a real aptitude for hooking up vacation and business travelers with flight schedules, affordable lodging, and tour deals. However, taking care of honeymooners and conventioneers doesn't get her to the office with a smile on her face. She knows she won't be a travel agent forever, but when Lorrie lands her first travel account with a rock band — she has stumbled upon a niche that pleases her rock 'n' roll soul.

Scenario No. 3: Bill, a carpenter, builds houses for a living. When he comes home at the end of a hard day, he doesn't reach for a six-pack and park himself in front of the TV. Instead, he can't wait to get to his workshop to get at his latest wood- or bone-carving project.

In college, Bill spent endless hours casting bronze and other sculptures in the school's foundry. Even as a carpenter, the artistic impulse manifested itself as Bill put intricate designs in his woodwork. One day, after years of carving Indian and animal motifs, he finds he's able to earn a living by selling his sculptures. Bill recognizes that his knowledge for wood-working and passion for sculpting have merged into a trade that he has mastered.

Glenn's passion was law enforcement; his knowledge was construction. Lorrie's love was rock 'n' roll concerts; her knowledge was travel. All three have fulfilled the equation: **KNOWLEDGE + PASSION = THE BUSINESS FOR YOU TO MASTER.**

THIS IS THE PROPER juncture to introduce my M.E.S.H. theory. M.E.S.H. stands for "Master, Expand, Sharpen, Hype."

It's amazing how many people will drudge through work all week at their day jobs, just to get home and start another project. The first thing they do on Saturday mornings is wake up early and head down to the craft store or Radio Shack to get the supplies to work on their hobbies. Whether it's sewing clothes or building ham radios, they love it. You have to love something in order to devote yourself to it. The same is true of your bread-and-butter (your day job). In order to succeed in the work place, you've got to pay your dues and learn your trade.

Let me share with you how I perfected my knowledge, wedded it to my passion, and came to **master** what has become my niche.

I apprenticed in general printing by working five years full-time after I graduated from high school. My employer specialized in standard printing: lithography, offset, and so on. I soon perfected a knowledge of printing. Without knowing it, I was building a solid foundation for starting my own business a few years down the road. I never expected to become a professional printer. Like many, I fell into the trade.

In high school, I was heavily involved in all aspects of community theater, from acting on stage to running the lighting above it. I was a drama club buff. At one point, there was a call for someone to take care of the printing for the posters and programs that advertised our plays. Naturally, I raised my hand, and with the help of a woman,

Mary Henessy, who worked for a local printer, I learned the basic tasks: simple paste-up, camera work, and so on. In addition to my other drama duties, I became the "print guy" for our high school theater productions.

After high school, with no work experience other than having been a restaurant busboy, I hoped to earn money for college. I was hired at a prestigious printing firm in town as an apprentice. I worked upstairs in the "grind," pasting books, typesetting, and performing dark-room duties in quarters so cramped I barely had head room. In backwards fashion, I embarked on a career in printing because of my theater interest.

During my five years as a junior printer, I'd go home at the end of the work day and head right into repertory theater work. I played Hamlet in "Rosencrantz and Guildenstern are Dead." I danced in five musicals. I handled lighting direction for Reno's annual "Sheep Dip" parody of community figures, sponsored by the Reno Ad Club. I manned the stage lights for local professional cover bands playing bars or lounges, and even a few school dances. I was involved in all aspects of the entertainment industry. And, of course, as a fan, I loved going to rock concerts. The latter provided me with inspiration.

With my printer's mind, I noticed there was a need for graphics and printing in the music industry. I decided to find out who exactly handled the print work for concerts — the tickets, the programs, and the security passes for those lucky ones who got to go backstage and meet the band.

To make a long story short, this is how I got into the business of graphic design and printing for the international touring industry: First, I secured a packet from a company that was a leading producer of backstage concert passes and similar credentials. (It took months of research in the library, looking through music industry publications such as Billboard and Variety, and running through the Yellow Pages of phone books from across the country, before I finally checked the flip side of a backstage pass and got the name of the company that produced it, in fine print at the bottom!)

Then I persuaded my employer to let me research the market and try to get customers. I spent six months, in my spare time, getting nowhere. No business. I persevered, however, because this line of work had by now grown into a palpable dream; it was something I knew I would love to be doing. What kept me going? What ultimately has led to my success? My business idea possessed the right chemistry.

KNOWLEDGE + PASSION = THE BUSINESS FOR YOU TO MASTER.
This is the "M" part of the M.E.S.H. theory.

NOW LET'S TALK ABOUT the "expand" part of M.E.S.H. This refers to expanding one's clientele to a national market.

Not every industry, field, or trade lends itself to developing business nationwide. There is enough business in most towns for plumbers. There's always enough business for a good personal injury lawyer or a gardening shop. One isn't going to become the expert from out of town by selling household furniture. Customers are satisfied with what's in their own city; they don't travel to St. Louis to patronize a furniture store.

Let's consider, instead, the scenario of an advertising executive who, every day after work, takes his metal detector and heads out on an excursion. He grows extremely adept at locating precious metals — veritable hidden treasures. He has his techniques down. He has mastered the craft. He ends up writing literature on how to excel at metal detecting. He also lectures at the local library and teaches a six-week course at the local YMCA. The response from students is gratifying.

Here is a skill unique enough, "niched" enough, if you will, in which to warrant becoming an out-of-town expert. There is certainly sufficient interest among the general population, but he'll have to **expand** his market. He'll need to expand his territory, whether it be regional (say, the West Coast) or national. In fact (hats off to you if you've already grasped the notion) our nascent metal detection maven must expand his market in order to present himself as an expert.

Image is the game, here. This budding expert may market himself as the West Coast's specialist in instructing metal detection, conducting seminars, offering private lessons, and holding weekend retreats centered around finding gold, jewels, antique nails, and wagon wheels along pioneer trails. So (and fortunately, for him, his advertising background helps him along) he publicizes his business all along the West Coast. Before long, he's holding workshops in Red Lion Inns up and down Washington, Oregon, and California.

Glenn, our expert jail-builder, must expand his market beyond his home town. (How many jails can be built in any one area?) Lorrie, the travel agent to the stars, must expand her market beyond her immediate terrain. And Bill, the wood-carver, must sell himself to the national scene; he'll be out of business practically before he starts if he tries to sell sculptures only to his townsfolk.

In my own case, I ended up expanding out of necessity. My first instincts had been to round up business locally. This was because my own community was all I was familiar with. Young and naive as I was, I had no grand design to go nationwide, so I hit the local sound and lighting stores, music clubs and bars. In no time at all I realized that I didn't have a big enough market. I had to expand it.

If you've absorbed anything from these initial chapters, I hope it is the following: this book is about reaching out and going further. It's not about staying in your home town and carving out a livable income. It's about **master**ing expertise in an area. It's about **expand**ing the vision of your customer base as you market that expertise. And right after that, it's about **sharpen**ing it.

BY SHARPEN, I MEAN focus. Concentrate your energy. Just as I had mastered printing, then expanded my market to a national level, I sharpened and focused on a particular client base: the entertainment touring industry. Instead of doing graphics and printing for every industry under the sun, I focused on pitching my expertise to a niche of the industry I loved. Concert tours filled the bill for me. The shows seemed absolutely magical. There was so much mystery behind the big productions and stages.

To be honest, much of my inspiration stemmed from my desire to get backstage, meet the stars, and see as many concerts as I could. Why not? Just to be able to tell people I worked for the Rolling Stones was a thrill. It is a very human motive. Our mythical travel agent will want to tell her cronies she's just booked the hotel rooms for the Flying Elvii. (Whether you're a specialized seamstress or architect, you will want to tell those in your circle whom you're working with, and the bigger, the better.)

I sharpened in on a specific market, and I found my niche. I didn't get greedy or overzealous. I didn't spread myself too thin. Similarly, our hypothetical travel agent focused on touring entertainers, not just a business person or family needing help with airline and room accommodations. Our wood carver didn't salivate over the prospects of building cabinets for every home in Lakeview, Oregon. And Glenn, our jail builder, didn't lie awake at night fantasizing about all the strip mall developers who might beckon his services.

There's a phrase I'll borrow from another source: K.I.S.S. It stands for: Keep It Simple, Stupid. Don't overextend yourself. You're becoming an expert, not a mercenary-for-hire. This book will help you **sharpen** your business plan by awakening in you your smarts and your heart. I might add that there is a methodical way to focus on what market may exist in your field of expertise. Investigate the industry where you've built your knowledge, and analyze the industry that relates to your passion. List all the different services that are needed by each of these industries. You'll be surprised at the infinite ways industries intersect. Among these intersections lies the right one for you.

Consider, for example, a professional football team. It needs a stadium to play in and someone to tend to the playing field and landscaping. The team needs someone to handle its food concessions, make and maintain the uniforms, service the team's buses, cart its luggage to and from airports, massage players' aching muscles, even provide all their Ben Gay.

Now, let's consider a man who loves football but goes into his father's tailoring business. It suits his acumen, and he becomes an expert at making suits. Why not take his sewing knowledge, merge it with his lifelong passion for football, and let him become a uniform designer? The intertwinings of industries are infinite.

In my case, I was a printer who recognized that the touring industry needed someone to do graphics and printing. Voila — there I was, a printer for the international touring industry. I'd sharpened in.

BEFORE YOU TAKE the plunge as an expert from out of town, before you quit your day job, you must investigate your niche. To do this you should turn into a little spy. You should investigate who does what in your industry. One way to investigate is to visit the library on a regular basis. Leaf through magazines that relate to the industries of your knowledge and/or passion.

I first went through music-industry publications such as Billboard, Variety, and the Hollywood Reporter. Such large circulation trade magazines often carry advertisements for smaller, more specialized ones. I found there was a trade magazine for rock concerts, and even one for booking agents. The library didn't carry either, since the circulation of these tiny trades was too small. I sent away for the trades and delved into their pages, seeking articles and advertisements that would clue me in to who exactly produced graphics and printing for concert tours. The hunt got me started.

There is a second way to investigate. If you have even just a modest amount of gumption, track down the telephone numbers of people you believe would be customers for businesses in your area of expertise. Inquire about who provides the services you want to provide. For example, the tailor with the passion for football could call the San Francisco 49ers to learn who designs their uniforms.

This tactic may require a number of calls and referrals, but the tailor will probably end up with enough information to begin networking. He may find there are 500 people already designing uniforms for sports teams. Then he'll have to do a little more searching for the right business to specialize in.

Lets not forget the Internet. Using this fast growing tool you will be able to locate serious competitors. I will expand on the Internet later in the book, however this is a nice quick way to do some searching. Using search engines on the World Wide Web you will be able to find other business related to or similar to the business you are thinking of.

I didn't know it at the time, but my difficulty in finding a concert goods printer should've sent me a positive signal. The other extreme, finding too many people already specializing in the niche you're aiming for, is a bad thing. If this is the case, you should abandon your idea and hunt for a new niche. (Finding zero people in your proposed niche is intriguing, but may also indicate there's no market for your intended specialty.)

The perfect amount is just a few specialists in your

niche. When you find out who they are, you should learn their products, prices, and clients. It could take you several weekends or even months of legwork, making calls and requests for brochures and other literature these businesses have. You may even have to pose as a customer.

Investigating your market is very necessary. I did my detective work the hard way. You should take advantage of any short-cuts that appear, via library, internet, and phone research. To my delight, there weren't very many people specializing in graphics or printing for the entertainment industry.

Ultimately, what every budding expert from out of town with a promising niche must realize is: there are not going to be a lot of competitors for this business you're creating. There are not going to be a lot of travel agents specializing in travel for entertainers. There are not going to be a lot of project managers building jails. There are not going to be many sculptors who are working exclusively producing Indian art in antler and wood. As for the few who are — they're going to be very surprised you found their niche.

THE FINAL STEP IN the M.E.S.H. theory is the **hype**, marketing and advertising yourself to ensure your industry knows about you. We'll discuss the hype part in detail later, starting with Chapter Six. Just remember for now that after mastering, expanding, and sharpening, you've got to make sure you market yourself, using all the available tools.

In sum, there is nothing mystical about my M.E.S.H. theory. It involves a logical and disciplined approach to becoming an expert from out of town. And it works. It can make you successful at doing work that you're good at and that you love.

Nearly all of us have early childhood dreams that never come to fruition. How can they? There aren't that many astronauts or ballerinas. Yet, that doesn't mean we ever lose our secret yearning for outer space or dance, nor should we. As we find ourselves developing skills in the trades we enter as adults, we should never let go of our passions. Consider the woman who wanted to become a singer, but instead developed an expertise in makeup. She could become one of the great makeup artists for the opera world!

You know you're on your way to success when you wake up in the morning, happy and eager to get going on the day's work. This is opposed to the poor souls jarred from sleep by the alarm clock. They drag themselves into the shower for yet another day in the "salt mines."

Shouldn't we love our jobs?

The next few chapters will address the proper attitude and strategy to forge ahead in a career as an expert from out of town. You'll notice it all involves implementing the M.E.S.H. theory.

CHAPTER FOUR
"Don't Psych Yourself Out"

At this stage, it is inevitable that self-doubt will creep in. It seems the more legwork you invest in developing a business idea, the more opportunities there are for pessimism to haunt you. Expect it, recognize it for what it is, and keep moving forward. Don't get psyched out!

The beast of doubt rears its ugly head in many different forms. I'll identify five of its incarnations in this chapter:
- The fear I dub, "The Teachers' Lounge Complex." (Perhaps its chief manifestation.)
- The fear of bad luck.
- The fear of nay-sayers.
- The fear of competition.
- The fear of risk-taking.

REMEMBER FOURTH GRADE? YOU'RE no longer a little tike; you sense you're on the edge of puberty. You've got new friends, you're communicating more with adults, you possess a budding sense of maturity.

One day, walking down the school's hall during recess, you catch a glimpse through a cracked door of the Teachers' Lounge. You linger for a few wide-eyed moments, staring into this mysterious and forbidden zone. It is a foregone conclusion among all your friends that the Teacher's Lounge is where the teachers meet to secretly plot their student-control strategies and share intelligence about particular troublemakers. The teachers are seen as one all-powerful group, all cooperating with each other, producing a united front. Each one knows everything there is to know about the others' students. The Teachers' Lounge is so off-limits to kids you half-believe that you'd be vaporized if you were to step across its threshold.

Surreptitiously standing at the door, you spy a refrigerator and microwave oven. This is surprising. Teachers eat, too? You notice a can of root beer. Students are not allowed soda in school. Then, to your great shock, a rather grave-looking, bearded science instructor whose appearance has always intimidated you, bumps his knee and utters a curse. Too late, you giggle. He turns toward the door. You are off down the hall toward the playground, barely able to digest what you've just witnessed.

THERE ISN'T A READER out there who hasn't experienced some form of Teachers' Lounge Complex. When we were young, our teachers seemed to be a superior species, but as we grew older, we came to know teachers we could even call our friends. Some of us even became teachers ourselves.

At some point, the aura was punctured. Teachers weren't one big clique. They weren't a well-organized coalition of omnipotent beings wielding absolute control. Many couldn't even stand each other. You realized they were mere mortals like the rest of us. They went home from school at the end of the day and had just as many problems to cope with as we did. The Teachers' Lounge was no Central Control; it was just another room.

Yet Teachers' Lounge Complex, the feeling that you are an outsider, a subordinate, persists in many forms. Consider the sentiments many Americans harbor these days against their government. They believe it to be some monolithic entity, self-perpetuating and continually seeking new ways to tighten control over its citizens. Conspiracy buffs have replaced the Teachers' Lounge with The Government.

The paranoia du jour in 1995 concerned so-called black helicopters purportedly surveying the citizenry and preparing the way for new world order in which a select few would rule. The fact that millions of Americans would have to be in on this dirty secret didn't seem to impress the mindset of the conspiracy crowd.

As anyone who has worked for the government knows, it is no more well-organized, efficient, or finely focused on the future than any enormous, far-flung corporation. Rather, "The Government" is composed of legions of pencil pushers, clock-watchers, cogs in the machine, career-minded yuppies, harried spouses, struggling singles, beer-guzzling bowlers, God-fearing church-goers, burned-out administrators, and simple, honest working folk, most of whom are as unclear about the inner workings of government, and even the relationship of their office with all the other myriad offices, as any tax-payer is. The Government is as much the person delivering your mail or digging a containment line around a forest fire as it is the long-winded lawmaker delivering a bewildering speech in Congressional Committee.

The Government is not the Teachers' Lounge. The Teachers' Lounge is not the Teacher's Lounge. There is no Teachers' Lounge. That is, except for a rather unremarkable room set aside for teacher's to take their breaks in. This is important to remind yourself as you embark on becoming an expert from out of town. Teachers' Lounges are sure to materialize in your mind as you expand your market nationwide. They are analogous to The Big City.

IN MY FIELD, FOR EXAMPLE, the public at large believes sex, drugs, and corruption are the rules of the trade. People may be greatly surprised how ordinary and mundane 99 percent of the world of entertainment really is. You find the same common people filling the same posts: secretaries, accountants, mid-level managers, and shipping clerks.

There isn't the sleaze and skullduggery that the tabloid media says there is.

"The Media." Believe it or not, the term media is a gross misnomer insofar as it conveys that all newspapers, tabloids, and magazines, radio stations, television stations, book publishers, movie companies, and billboard advertisers are somehow in cahoots, delivering coordinated information. As hard-bitten veteran journalists may tell you, most story assignment editors haven't got a clue what makes news beyond their gut instincts. One thing they do know is that the public has an overblown fascination with celebrities, entertainers, and athletes. In other words, the public has a version of Teachers' Lounge Complex when it comes to stars. The tabloids take full advantage by feeding off of it.

What I found out as I filled a niche in the entertainment world was that stars are people, too. After having met Mick Jagger, Billy Joel, and numerous other marquee-toppers, I realized they are actually human, too. Certainly they have proved extremely aggressive and motivated to do well for themselves — that's why they made it where they are. They are not intimidated by the "Teacher's Lounge" of the worldwide market. Perhaps their greatest trait is that they are excellent business people. Not ultimate party monsters.

Those around them aren't engaged in some daily movable feast of sex, drugs, and payoffs. Even the backstage areas at their concerts aren't some makeshift Sodom and Gomorra. Backstage is rather boring. You'll often find a banquet table with cold cuts and soft drinks and maybe a few local radio disc jockeys trying to mix with musicians and management aides.

As for sleaze, just once in my ten-year career was I offered a kickback from someone who offered to toss business my way. I turned him down and that was that. The rest of the time it's been business as usual: sending potential customers sample packets of my graphics and printing, handling orders, making sure deadlines are met, products are delivered, and bills are collected.

Those who ply their trades in the entertainment world are for the most part a bunch of honest, hard-working people trying to feed their families. Just like the rest of us. It's the same in the advertising world and the sporting world, and the investment world, and the world of politics. It's the same in the great expanse of marketing territory outside your home town.

One reason most business operators and entrepreneurs never expand their markets beyond their home turf is because they're afraid of leaving their comfort zones. They're timid about going out of town because it seems big and scary to them. This is just another example of Teachers Lounge Complex - the fear of the unknown, the sense that superhumans roam like dinosaurs beyond the pale.

To go forward, you must recognize your self-doubts for what they are, and continue on. You will become the expert from out of town. You will discover the terrain is hardly foreign at all — just a larger fish bowl than the one you're in. Whenever these feelings of being an unworthy outsider crop up, put yourself back in fourth grade, standing at the door of the Teachers' Lounge, gaining your first inkling that these all-powerful, unapproachable beings are, in fact, rather ordinary. Consider the new circles you're entering as merely strange terrain about to become demystified.

LET'S TALK ABOUT A second incarnation of the beast of self-doubt: dread of bad luck.

Some people think the only way they'll succeed is if they "get lucky," if they somehow end up "in the right place at the right time." Perhaps this is true for those who win the lottery, but not for anyone else.

Joseph Addison, the great English essayist and statesman of the late 17th and early 18th centuries, wrote: "I never knew an early rising, hard working, prudent man, careful of his earnings and strictly honest, who complained of hard luck."

It is true some successful people will claim their accomplishments are merely the product of having gotten "lucky." This, however, is often their way of putting a person at ease, by diminishing feelings of envy. If you truly think it's going to take a stroke of luck to succeed as an expert from out of town — forget about the entire thing. Go back to your regular job tomorrow morning at 8 o'clock, and be satisfied. The fact is, there is no such thing as "luck." The French have a saying: "Heaven helps those who help themselves." Another way of saying it is: "You make your own luck." I like to think of it this way: A lucky person is someone who doesn't believe in luck.

Let's return briefly to the Teachers' Lounge Complex. The student who politely knocks on the door and finds a teacher to answer an important question is not "lucky" to get an answer. The student set himself or herself up to get the answer by not being intimidated by his or her surroundings. The student made the right connection. The same will be true for you as you become the expert from out of town. As you drive into a strange city to build new business contacts, or communicate with people from across the country via the Internet, you'll develop your business niche not through luck but by placing yourself, through diligent effort, in "the right place at the right time."

NOW TO DISCUSS A third manifestation of self-doubt: Beware the nay-sayers. These are the critics who are always shooting down your dreams and heaping sarcasm and scorn on your announced business plans. They try, without openly saying so, to sabotage your spirit. It is important to distinguish between the nay-sayers and those who will actually prove valid sounding boards. Do not confuse the two, for both will appear as you take the practical step of bouncing your ideas off others.

As you develop your plan, you will benefit greatly from testing your notions out on others. They can provide excellent feedback. Developing a business plan can be a lonely journey. Harnessing the interest, and even enthusiasm, of others helps you build energy and keeps you moving along.

So get out there and get information, get as much as you can. Talk to as many people as seems appropriate. Test out your idea. You'll absorb the good advice and ignore the bad advice, with a polite smile. Just beware the nay-sayers, whose sole purpose is delivering the negative word.

Inevitably, family members will become part of the discussion, whether a parent, spouse, or in-law. Let them know that you're going ahead with your business plan. What you would appreciate from them is constructive input. Ultimately, however, your most constructive sounding boards will be people already working in the industry. They're the ones familiar with the lay of the land and can truly steer you in profitable directions. You may end up buying lunch for lots of people, but it will prove a most valuable investment. Collect what you can at the outset.

Glenn the prospective jail-builder will court counsel from veteran contractors and from correctional experts. Lorrie the would-be travel agent to touring musicians will seek out entertainment acts and travel agency owners. Bill, who plans to go full-tilt into carving original wood sculptures will talk to self-supporting artists and gallery owners. Some of the feedback may encourage them greatly; some of it may cause them to rethink their initial plans. Both types of feedback should be welcomed.

Remember Aesop's Fables? There is the tale of the mule and his master returning home at the end of the day. As they walk down a narrow and precipitous mountain road, the mule gazes down a cliff and spies his stall at the bottom. Convincing himself the quickest and easiest way home is via the most direct route, he starts over the edge. His master grabs the foolish beast's tail and orders him to halt, but the mule will have none of that. Finally the man lets go and the mule tumbles head over heels down the mountainside.

The morale: Those who ignore friendly advice are doomed to disaster.

THERE IS A WORLD of difference between helpful advice and deliberately harmful (and useless) advice. Consider Glenn spilling the beans about his business plan to his buddies at the Tuesday night bowling league. Naturally, he ends up the butt of jokes. The advice he gets is their type of advice:

"Ah, you're crazy. You should appreciate what you've got. You've got a good contracting business going."

And: "If you were going to strike it rich, buddy, you would've made it by now." And: "How do you expect to become a big-time national contractor when you're stuck here in Arizona?"

Glenn's beer-drinking, bowling buddies have fun with him. Why should he have to put himself through such torment? None in this group was in any way connected to specialty contracting. They could barely afford bail if they were brought to one of the jails Glenn built. Instead, Glenn would do well to look up the editor of, say, "Concrete Today" magazine, and run his business idea past him. Trade magazines are a fertile ground for specialized expertise. If you can break through your Teachers' Lounge Complex about the publishing world, you're on your way to exploiting this resource.

A FEW FINAL THOUGHTS on nay-sayers. I can almost guarantee that if you talk to people who are extremely successful at what they do, they will be enthusiastic about your idea. These are the golden souls who live to create, whose minds are always turning over ideas. Successful people see the seeds of success in other people's ideas. Conversely, you're going to find very few nay-sayers who are, themselves, successful. They're not the type of people to take a risk. Once you get a negative response, go home and analyze it. Before you decide whether the negative input is worthy of deep thought, write down who gave the response, what the person's accomplishments are, and why you respect this person. It may be that the source is not someone whose input should be valued, and therefore, the negativity is not such a bad thing.

I ran into a lot of nay-sayers as I embarked on my enterprise of providing graphics and printing for the entertainment industry. The local owner of the sound and lighting company nearly shot me out of the saddle when he told me he "they deal with the big boys." Instead of letting discouragement get the best of me, what I should have done was ask myself: Who is this person? How has he succeeded? What is his reputation? Should I listen to this person, or shouldn't I? I temporarily succumbed to The Teachers' Lounge Complex — cowed by him being an entertainment insider, an inhabitant of a world where I didn't belong.

So when it comes to the bona fide nay-sayers — it is important to realize there is something wrong with them, not you. Our minds are programmed as children with negative reinforcements, what we can't do. These negative thought patterns threaten to replay over and over like a broken record throughout the course of our lives. I recommend very few books to my readers, but one I do suggest you buy is, "What to Say When You Talk to Yourself," by Shad Helmstetter (Pocket Books, copyright 1982).

"What to Say When You Talk to Yourself" is not a self-help book, per se. If you don't read the book, you should at least know that its central point is the commandment to think positively. If you tell yourself over and over that you're going to do something, the odds are dramatically increased that you're going to do it. The only person who has control over yourself is you. Whether it be waking up early, getting along with your mate, or building a successful business — tell yourself you have succeeded, and chances are you will. Become your own "yea-sayer."

I found this quote from Mark Twain the evening I was finishing this book and had to add his words of wisdom regarding advice from people:

"Keep always from people who try to belittle your ambitions. Small people always do that, but the really great people make you feel that you, too, can become great."

WE MUST DISCUSS A fourth variety of self-doubt: Fear of competition. Do not, I repeat, do not waste your time and energy worrying about competitors. Instead, learn from them, at least at the beginning.

Let's return for a moment to Lorrie the incipient travel agent for entertainers. Seeking constructive advice from an insider in the world of entertainers, she has overcome her Teachers' Lounge Complex about the magazine world, and prepares to make a call to the editor of Variety magazine, located in Los Angeles.

As Lorrie readies to dial the phone number of the editorial office listed in a front page of the magazine, a chilling thought flashes into her mind: what if she's letting the cat of the bag? What if she's giving away her hot idea to someone who could beat her into the market? What if the editor writes about Lorrie's brilliant plan, and before she can even get started, she's beaten out of the box by 50 other would-be tour trip-setters? Lorrie need not fret. Chances are slim to none that the magazine editor is in travel, and the odds even smaller that the editor is going to run out and start on a plan to become a specialty travel agent.

Secondly, it's highly unlikely this editor is going to somehow broadcast Lorrie's idea to the world. In the remote likelihood the idea does get spread around, and some other travel agent does get the notion to test the waters in Lorrie's prospective niche — then good! The more such businesses that start out, the more the market will be developed.

We are not talking here about securing a patent on an invention, or a copyright on a song, or a trademark. Those are business ideas that need to be kept under wraps until legal protection is secured. Developing a niche to serve as an expert from out of town is impossible to keep as a secret for very long. It is inevitable that as Lorrie finally initiates her plan and builds a clientele, others with her qualifications will hear about it and consider following her lead.

Think of it this way: How many will follow? To accomplish anything requires three stages: thinking of it, acting upon it, and succeeding at it. Almost every travel agent who will catch wind of Lorrie's new specialty and even seriously entertain thoughts of trying the same thing, will never actually lift a finger to do so. As for those who do try, most will strike out somewhere between the investigation phase and the enactment phase. After all, hard, hard work is involved.

As for the extremely minute number who may develop into experts from out of town in Lorrie's particular niche — good for them. Nobody can capture an entire market. Competition is very healthy. It makes you work harder, and work smarter. Competition motivates.

One should not squander a minute of time and energy worrying about prospective competition! It is a negative thought. It is a nay-sayer's thought. Its only result will be to psych you out. There are corporations in this country with sizable divisions charged with nothing but trying to pay attention to the competition. All that energy could be put to better use, in new product research, in better development.

YOU MUST THINK POSITIVE! It's a lesson you might have to relearn over and over again. When I first conceived of writing this book, I went to the library to research whether similar books had been published. I was very scared to ask the librarian at the reference desk to search for the title, "The Expert From Out of Town."

How neurotic of me! This woman wasn't going to scribble down the title of my planned book, then run home to write her own manuscript. She wouldn't even have known what I was talking about. I was foolishly victimizing myself psyching myself out, at the very start. I soon got over it, and was unafraid to walk into any library or bookstore and inquire whether it had a book titled along the lines of, "The Expert From Out of Town."

Remember this: if you're worrying about your competition, you're going to scare yourself. If you don't overcome this worry, you'll be ultimately hurting your customers. Why? Because you'll tend to not freely circulate or publicize your catalogs, your pamphlets, and all the information you need to give out on demand. You'll be too paranoid about competitors getting hold of such information. You'll worry about them stealing your ideas and figuring out ways to undercut your prices or glom onto your market base. This fear will make you shortchange your legitimate customers.

Lorrie's prospective clients will want to know what her working arrangements are, what backup plans are in place, what her fees are, and how long the itineraries will take to be completed. If Lorrie holds back on providing any such information — for fear she's being interviewed by a potential rival — she may be losing a legitimate customer. It's a bad practice to get into. If Lorrie has a solid business idea and puts the proper work into it — it will succeed. She should direct her energies to developing her business and taking care of her customers, not worrying about her competitors. The name of the game, friends, is taking care of your customers.

Let me qualify this slightly. It is suggested that

when you start your business plan, you should contact businesses that are competitors, to gather information from them. They're not going to know who you are. There's nothing wrong with it. It's healthy. As I focused in on entering the business of producing graphics and printing for the international touring industry, I zeroed in on the company that was the largest provider, and arranged to receive a sample packet. Once I gathered enough information about the company's services, I got to work on building and serving my own clients.

Today, I'm focused entirely on my customers, on new products and developments, and I'm not looking over my shoulder to see what the other guy's doing. Once a year, I may take a week to check up on my counterparts, to see if I'm still competitive, but believe it or not, as an expert from out of town you're going to find out more about your competition through your customers than by checking yourself. If someone else has come up with a good product or new technology, your clients are going to tell you about it. They may wonder, for example, if you can provide the same service. If you devote energies into your customers, it pays off in more ways than one. In sum: don't worry about your competition. Let them worry about you.

LET'S TALK ABOUT ONE final fear: The fear of taking a risk.

History is littered with spectacular failures who bounced back to unbelievable successes. We needn't list them all here, but students of American history can read up on presidents Washington, Lincoln, and Truman; writers "O. Henry" and Hemingway; and just about any scientist, inventor, or athlete.

You want astounding business disasters? Try automobile pioneer Henry Ford, bankrupt before building an empire and revolutionizing his industry. What about the young Walt Disney, reportedly axed by an advertising agency for a "singular lack of drawing ability." Can you believe it?! Their stories should provide perspective. Even the great "fail" and their setbacks are hardly death knells.

Sometimes losing a job can be the best thing that ever happened to you. I know this was true in my case. I lost a job at one point, but I was able to brush myself off and get back on my feet. Two years later, my former employers wanted me to buy them out. I turned them down, of course. My own prospering business was keeping me more than busy, and does to this day.

Here's a story from the world of corporate giants. At 38, Sergio Zyman found himself the head of U.S. marketing for Coca-Cola. He'd made a name for himself by introducing the enormously successful Diet Coke. So in 1984, the Mexican native decided he would daringly reverse his company's two-decade market-share decline to arch-rival Pepsi-Cola. What Zyman would do was replace century-old Coke with a better-tasting formula: New Coke. New Coke was introduced in April 1985, and it proved such a disaster, the "Edsel" of the soft-drink industry, that the old formula reappeared on the market — as Coca-Cola Classic — in only 79 days.

Zyman was gone a year later, his career as an executive seemingly as dead as a 3,000-year-old mummy. But experts will tell you that the most successful business people don't ever entertain the idea of failure. Sure, they'll suffer mishaps, but they never consider these to be crash-and-burn nose-dives. Rather, they regard stumbles and tumbles as merely the temporary, and perhaps inevitable, awkwardnesses to whether as they continue forward toward their goals. In fact, many view "false starts" in a positive light — as necessary learning experiences. To them, failure is a great teacher. Rather than discouraging, it is encouraging. Here's another secret: they understand that failure often foreshadows success.

Consider this: when all was said and done after the

debacle of New Coke, Coca-Cola — buoyed by the reintroduction of Classic Coke — enjoyed the largest-ever one-year rise in product sales! As for SeÒor Zyman: after leaving Coke, he started a consulting business. For seven years, he advised such corporate giants as Microsoft, Miller Brewing, and, in time . . . Coca-Cola. In 1993, Coke wooed Zyman back to the fold and gave him expanded executive powers! The reason? His risk-taking mentality was in great demand.

SUCCESSFUL BUSINESS PERSONS are never fatalistic. They are always optimistic. They continue through the maze, patiently and expectantly, until they find the right path. You have got to accept risk as a component of your overall campaign. Becoming the expert from out of town won't all be clear sailing. There is always the chance the ship will go down in a storm. But if it happens, you must build a new ship.

As you confront your fears of failure, ask yourself this: "What's the worst thing that can happen?" Dale Carnegie courses have taught this very same tactic for years. Go ahead, write down the worst thing that can happen if your business doesn't at first succeed.

I'm not telling you to go quit your day job yet. I'm not telling you to take an absurd risk before you've properly laid the groundwork to go full-tilt into a new business. I'm saying you can find a few customers and complete jobs for them on the side, and build up your financial reserves, before you make your big move. Do it if you decide you must. Err on the side of prudence. What I am telling you is that for those with the proper mindset, success is only a matter of time. That includes someone like you — a budding expert from out of town.

CHAPTER FIVE
"Stay Where You Are"

"An expert is a man from another city. And the farther away the city is, the greater the expert."

I pulled this anonymous quotation from "Speakers Encyclopedia," a 40-year-old book I keep in my office at home. I recommend you write this quote out and tape it to your refrigerator. The wisdom embedded in these words should be firmly engraved upon your brain cells. You are now on your way to becoming the expert from out of town.

While it may seem paradoxical, you become the expert from out of town by staying *exactly where you are.* This is because you will be developing a market outside your area. As I have mentioned in previous chapters, the strategy of keeping your headquarters in your home town flies in the face of advice you are sure to receive from certain parties who would love to bestow you with counsel at the outset. Such "deep thinkers" will staunchly assert, as if logic were their middle name, that you must leave town and relocate to "where the action is," in most cases a big city. Of course, logic dictates that to be the "out-of-town" expert you must remain based outside the markets you will be targeting.

"*. . . And the farther away the city is, the greater the expert.*"

Some time ago, I was in Lakeview, Oregon, a pleasant little town south-east of Portland. I must have talked to ten young adults in bars, stores, and on the street. Everyone of them was trying to get out of Lakeview! They were all on their way out of town. They were all going to leave and "make something of themselves." Sound familiar? It should. Most of us have "Lakeviews" somewhere in our backgrounds.

We have to remember here that the advantage of being the expert from out of town is that you're out of town. So don't put any energy into thinking you have to move to Los Angeles. Move to Los Angeles, New York, or Seattle, and you'll become just one of the thousands. All you'll become is just one more of the same-sized fish in a much, much larger pond. You'll have blown the whole theory! I can't say this enough: Stay put.

LET ME CONTINUE FOR a bit about Lakeview. It seems unfortunate that deeply embedded in the psyche of 20th Century Americans is the ideal of striking out for the big city, wooed like moths by the bright lights. Many of us have seen the same pattern unfold in the lives of earnest young people with stars in their eyes. They leave town full of dreams of striking it rich in a larger city . . . and inevitably return, prodigal sons and daughters having struck out.

I couldn't begin to list all the people I've known from my involvement in community theater in Reno who were going to become actors or actresses in the Big City. They were hell-bent on getting out of Reno. They'd gotten it into their minds that in order to succeed they had to be Somewhere Else. Each and every one of them was committing a classic mistake. They failed to recognize: you are what you are, where you are.

If you are going to wake up at the same time, have the same attitude and the same level of expertise in Portland, Oregon, as you are in Lakeview, Oregon, you're going to end up with no better than the same level of success. Your IQ, talent, or drive are not going to magically increase simply by moving to a larger population center! At the same time, your problems and your bad habits, are not going to somehow disappear. In fact, your defects may become magnified in strange surroundings. The probability is that you will wind up right back where you came from, with two months or even two years spent learning a lesson about life.

This isn't the same as situating yourself in a healthy environment. If you're hanging around with a bunch of partiers or drunks in your Lakeview, then get away from them. Move to another area of town. This isn't to say you shouldn't situate yourself in a nurturing environment to get your training. Chances are you won't have the vocational or collegiate opportunities available in Lakeview that you will in Portland, or Seattle, or San Francisco. To learn to play jazz, you want the best music school you can find. Learning the ropes in jazz clubs in San Diego or New Orleans may be the thing to do for a time. But that's the educational phase. What we're addressing here is the post-mastering phase.

As a budding expert from out of town, all you actually need from your home area are telephone lines, Federal Express and/or United Parcel Service, and a major airport no more than a few hours away. All these are standard in most cities and towns in the America of the 1990s. So ask yourself, as someone who has mastered his or her trade, what purpose is served by leaving friends, family, and connections, just to head off to the city for the sake of moving to the Big City"? For you will still have the same behavior patterns in the Big City as you did in Lakeview.

I once insulted someone without meaning to. I was at a party for a young woman who aspired to make it big on the stage, and was moving out of Reno. If I wasn't exactly filled with great expectations for catching her name lighting up a marquee some day, it was because she happened to be approximately the tenth person from my circle of community theater veterans who was moving out of "The Biggest Little City in the World," as Reno's slogan goes, for one of the bigger cities of the world.

This particular starlet-to-be was moving to Boston to continue with repertory theater. As we bade her farewell, a book was passed around to be signed with such inscriptions as, "To success!" or, "You're moving on, we'll miss you," or, "No guts, no glory!" Blah blah blah.

When the book came to me, I declined, saying, "Well, you're going to be back in two months, anyway." The young woman's eyes flashed homicidal. I really hadn't meant to be rude. I guess I can't help myself, sometimes. Needless to say, she was back in Reno in two months. The point is this: whether you're a business entrepreneur, writer or thespian, you can nurture your talent and build up your experience while continuing to base yourself in your town of origin.

Reno has an airport, train station and bus station, and is situated on two major highways. There's no hindrance to an actor or actress being based in the "Biggest Little City" while auditioning for parts in other locales. In fact, there will be more mystique about you coming from Reno, or Carson City, or Elko than, say, Southern California. The Hollywood agents would love to boast about discovering a star-to-be in a little town deep in Nevada. It will be exciting to them! They've seen enough gorgeous young waiters and waitresses, the so-called "Y and B," (young and beautiful) eager for a break in Tinsel Town.

The beauty about the "expert from out of town" theory is that it applies to so many industries. The musician from out of town to the actor from out of town. As for the particular young actress who bombed out in Boston and came back to Reno, I have good news to report: She is leaving town again. While living again in Reno, she auditioned for a part in San Diego. Now she is moving there, and I know she is going to succeed. The reason? She's already failed somewhere else. She learned her lesson. She came back home, realized she could market herself from Reno, and worked even harder at her craft. Now she's going to San Diego, job in hand. Little does she know, directors viewed her differently because she was from Reno, not Boston. They obviously saw her talents, her knowledge, her passion, come out. Ultimately, she has experienced the expert from out of town phenomenon, and doesn't even realize it.

ONCE YOU'VE SETTLED ON staying in town, there is one trap you must avoid. You are not to squander time and energy in a futile campaign aimed at milking the hometown market. Ignore this advice, and in time you will find yourself burned out on networking at the local Chamber of Commerce. I guarantee it.

Every decent-sized city or town has its Chamber, its Rotary Club, its Kiwanis Club, and so forth. I'm not knocking these civic and service organizations. (In fact, I'm a member of Rotary.) They fill a much-needed philanthropic purpose. Small business owners need these networks. After all, some businesses are meant to be local: the video store, the furniture store, the stereo warehouse. Their proprietors should be active in the local business circle; it's whom they do business with.

It's an entirely different story for the expert from out of town. Your whole angle is positioning yourself in the national market. So avoid Chamber of Commerce purgatory! Life as the Chamber carousel turns means finding out what function is on tap each month, where to go, dressing right, loading up with business cards . . . and then jostling with every other eager beaver who attends such affairs for the sole purpose of drumming up more business. That's the whole idea of Chamber functions — they are nothing more than networking feeding frenzies. The comical aspect is everyone is there to feed off everyone else.

What you would find at your first Chamber mixer is a bunch of people selling something, with nary a buyer among them. The affair will be held at a post-work, pre-dinner hour, at a local restaurant where banquet tables laid out with spicy chicken wings, celery sticks, and containers of blue cheese have been set up, next to a no-host bar.

You would have your insurance agent, your printer, your accountant, and your banker. You would have the person who runs the local travel agency, and the woman who is the "local guru" of planning parties and events. Everyone would still be dressed in nice work clothes, with their game faces on, schmoozing up a storm. Older members introduce newcomers around. Hands are shaken. Chatter is exchanged. People look constantly over each others' shoulders, keeping hungry eyes out for better targets of opportunity.

In Chamber of Commerce purgatory, you network to get introduced to people. Later, armed with tenuous contacts, you pound the pavement, knock on doors, make cold calls. Oh, you try so hard! You feel that if you can only break through with these folk you see at every Chamber mixer, and cultivate them as customers or contacts, you'll build your business into a sure success. But you won't, because to them you're nothing special. I've found this out the hard way. The people you'll meet at the local chamber mixer would rather look out of town to hire a specialist than go with you. They prove this truism every day, in every town. So don't bother with them!

A SIMPLE APPLICATION OF mathematics clinches this discussion about eschewing the local market. To illustrate, let's return briefly to our prototypical artist-expert from out of town, Bill the wood-carver. Bill joins the Chamber. He attends his first mixer. He meets the insurance salesman — who wants to sell him protection since he'll need it for his wood-carving career. The local special events planner wants Bill to throw a party to let everyone in town know about his new business. "It'll be exciting, and you'll make so many wonderful contacts," she chirps. The accountant wants to peddle his bookkeeping. "Don't try to do it yourself, the software's no good," he confides.

In time, it dawns on Bill that the travel agent is the only person whose business he'll need to engage — to leave town! Bill, of course, didn't have to attend this mixer to meet the travel agent; he could have looked her up in the Yellow Pages. A bit bewildered, memories of saliva sprayed in his face and bone-crushing hand grips from the overly assertive, Bill returns home that night with nine business cards stuffed in his pockets, and he realizes he hasn't given out any of his own.

Bill realizes there's no market for him in town. The first notion that enters his mind? "I've got to move." But this is backwards thinking. Bill doesn't need to leave town. He needs to market out of town. Bill needs to stay put and go find his customers outside the local market.

It's all a matter of percentages. If Bill lives in a town of 200,000 people, and aims to have 200 clients to make his business thrive, he'd have to gun for one in a thousand — a tenth of one percent (.10) — of his area's population base. One in every 1,000 people would have to become a customer. But if Bill expands to a market of 200 million, the odds change dramatically. He needs only look for one in a million — one ten-thousandth of one percent (.0001) — to become a customer. By going nationwide, Bill has increased his chances of landing customers a thousand-fold.

Once you go out of town, you're going to magnify your odds of finding customers by quantum leaps. Once you've found your niche and sharpened in on your focus, stay out of town. Develop your market there. You won't need to squander any time at the local Chamber to build up clientele. If anything, Chamber members will begin to come to you.

After you've gained a measure of success as the

expert from out of town, that's when you should hit a Chamber mixer, if you so desire. You may very well find that you make contacts more easily and effortlessly, for you now have a good feeling about yourself and your accomplishments. You will be happy and relaxed. You will look better and come across better than you did as a hungry entrepreneur on the prowl for potential customers. Your aura will be different.

Again, business is not meant to be as hard as you may think it is. It does, however, become difficult when you limit your market, therefore, expand it!

RECALL THE M.E.S.H. THEORY. What will really help Bill get moving on developing his out-of-town market — to sharpen — is when he lands his first out-of-town customer. This is a watershed event in the career of every expert from out of town. When Bill finds his first out-of-town buyer, his marketing strategy will be miraculously revealed to him.

Your first customer is your Rosetta Stone, your magic decoder ring. That person provides you the breakthrough formula, the secret recipe. Your first customer is the most important you will ever have, for he or she is your key to succeeding as an expert from out of town. I cannot express this strongly enough: when you land your first customer, take notes! Write down everything that got you to this person, and everything about this person. These are the precise clues to how you will find all your next customers.

It's all like building a detective's dossier. Take down the person's name, age, where he or she lives, his or her industry title, employer, income level, type of business, and interest in your service. Note well how this person heard about you (or vice versa). Was it via direct-mail marketing? Word-of-mouth? Through a trade publication?

Many experts from out of town will find that the

most critical information about their first customer could very well be the person's industry title. You're building what's known as a customer profile. This proved to be the case for me.

I wanted to become a printer and graphic designer for the international touring industry, but I had no clue where to begin looking for clients. Such is the first major hurdle every budding expert from out of town will face. I first tried concert promoters, the people who line up cash and venues and sign acts to perform. I sent out letters and sample packets of my products. I made telephone calls. I got zero response. I continued blindly, casting about through the strata of the entertainment industry. I contacted secretaries, record company executives, and music industry lawyers. I spent months trying to get in touch with booking agents. No one replied to my packages. No one returned my phone calls. I got absolutely nowhere. I was discouraged.

Little did I know, the deafening silence had absolutely nothing to do with bad product design, inadequate literature, or poor communication skills. I had all the tools. There was only one reason no one got back to me. They weren't responsible for buying what I was offering. They weren't the ones in charge of ordering the posters and programs, tickets and security credentials. The only reason I couldn't get anyone to return my calls was that I wasn't calling the right people!

I should have been trying to reach a creature known in the touring industry as the band's management company. It is the management company that decides who does the printing and graphics for tours. In fact, I came to learn, the management company has quite a big say in hiring almost every member of tour production, from the lighting companies to the carpenters to the wardrobe people to the publicist. It was only by trial and error that I finally made a right connection.

One day, I took a gamble. As I mentioned in Chapter

One, Billy Joel was booked for Lawlor Events Center, the primary concert arena in Reno. I headed up Virginia Street and dropped my package off at the front security desk. The package was passed on to Bobby Thrasher, Joel's production person. When I returned to the office from my lunch break, several messages awaited me.

That day was the first time I'd ever hit the target. Ironically, in my misdirected marketing in the months beforehand, I'd unwittingly come close to getting samples to band management, without knowing it. From that day forth, when I connected with Bobby Thrasher, I knew what targets to zero in on. It was a revelation to me of staggering proportions. The same will hold true for you, once you've reeled in your first customer.

Your initial marketing phase will likely be the most discouraging period of building your business. It will be a mighty wall to scale. If you get absolutely no response from the people you first contact, know that it is likely because they are not "in your industry." It is as if you were trying to sell apples to the dairy section, even though both produce and milk products are sold in the supermarket. Rest assured that the reason people won't get back to you at first is almost certainly not because you're not selling yourself well enough. Nine times out of ten, you're not selling to the right people!

Remember this: as an expert, you have a very tightly focused niche. When you do get in touch with the right parties, the ones empowered to hire you or purchase your work, they'll be very receptive. They'll be receptive because you're an expert, and because you're that mystique-laden entity, the expert from out of town.

LET'S RETURN TO BILL the wood-carver. He wants to market his hand-carvings, but he isn't sure whom his clientele will be. He joins his local Chamber of Commerce, attends a mixer, and reaps as his reward a pocketful of business cards. Want to know how he finds his first customer? Through a friend, Bill hears about a reporter who covers art for the Portland daily newspaper. Bill goes to the library and leafs through the past few weeks worth of issues, hunting down the reporter's by-line and familiarizing himself with her stories. Then he calls the reporter and leaves several messages on her voice mail. She eventually calls Bill back and they get to talking. Bill explains his business. "You know, I may have just the guy for you," the reporter eventually says. "He's a gallery owner outside Portland. I've written about him, and he's one of the foremost collectors of rare Northwest Indian art outside of a museum. I don't think he'll mind you calling, but let me call him first. If he's interested, I'll get back to you with his name and number."

This the reporter does. Bill returns to the library and obtains a copy of the article the reporter had written about this gallery owner. The owner's name is Herb Sawyer. Bill makes the call and introduces himself. He and Sawyer have a pleasant conversation.

One good thing that came out of Bill's attendance at the chamber mixer was that he met the town's printer as well as the owner of a small advertising agency. Bill invested some money and had a decent, four-color brochure produced with information about his business, plus photographs of his artwork and himself.

Bill mails Sawyer a brochure. He doesn't' hear back for a couple of weeks, then makes a follow-up call. Sawyer is apologetic. He had been vacationing in Mexico. "Want to get together next week? I should be free Tuesday."

Bill says he must consult his calendar. He cups the receiver, waits ten seconds, then says casually, "Yeah, it'll work. See you on the 22nd." Bill ends up driving up to the collector's gallery, in an upscale Portland suburb. They hit it off., and Bill has his first major buyer.

Howdy, Ted! This is Joe Bob, remember the
hay I lent you for the chamber function...
Well I was wondering if you could call your
friend, George, in Washington...

Back home, he takes good notes on everything he
can about Herb Sawyer. He writes down all the pertinent
information, and tapes it to the wall of his office. Sawyer is
a wealthy retired businessman, 66, who dabbles in hand
carvings himself, but fancies himself foremost as a historian
of Pacific Northwest history, primarily indigenous tribes.
His wife, Arthada, is also a fan of wood carvings. Bill has
made a quantum leap in identifying his customer base.

A FEW FINAL WORDS, first, on creating the aura
of the expert from out of town. Once you finally lock in on
potential customers, you must sell yourself firmly as the
authority in your field.

I didn't approach Billy Joel's manager and say, "I'm
interested in getting involved in the touring business." What
a mistake that would have been! No, I was a specialist in the

international touring industry. I was ready and eager to take on Billy Joel's account.

When Bill the wood-carver introduces himself to Herbert Sawyer, he doesn't do so with the bashful air of a neophyte. Bill is the master at his craft! "Hello, Mr. Sawyer, my name is William Gerber and I understand you collect Northwest Indian carvings," he begins. "I'm a master woodcarver known for my intricate original sculptures, and I was told by an arts journalist in Portland that this is the sort of artwork you're always keeping an eye out for."

Stand in front of a mirror and repeat 20 times a day: "I am an expert (insert your niche)." Believe it, for it is so.

Now, for a last word on networking: it works in mysterious ways. There is the theory that everyone on this

Hi, George? This is Ted, I have a friend...

Hi, John? This is George, can I ask a favor?

planet knows everyone else through a maximum of four or five connections. For example, I now know Billy Joel's production person, Bobby Thrasher, who knows many of the other management people of big-time touring industry. Therefore, through Bobby Thrasher, I became connected to everyone with whom I needed to be in my industry.

In Bill's case, he didn't know a Herb Sawyer even existed. By acting on a tip through his friend (first connection), he called up the newspaper reporter (second connection) and ended up in contact with Sawyer. Through three connections, Bill found his man. The point is, use your connections. Use someone to get to someone else and continue up the ladder.

Once you've gained your first customer, dissect him or her into demographic and psychographic parts. That's how you develop the prototype for identifying everyone else in the country who is a potential customer for you — the expert from out of town.

"An expert is an ordinary man away from home."

CHAPTER SIX
"Going Nationwide With Networking"

Now you've netted your very first customer. You have the profile fully fleshed out. Let's talk about capitalizing on this terrific chunk of intelligence by using it to find every other person in the country who matches the identifying qualities of your clientele.

Sound daunting? It won't be if you approach the task in workmanlike manner. There is no magic formula. What's involved is a lot of trial and error, but it's the indispensable portion of assembling your marketing campaign. I am talking about constructing your customer base.

Yes, it will be hard work. You should wish, however, that it were even harder. For this is one of the major bridges to cross that separates the wannabes from the actual experts from out of town. What it basically comes down to is networking. You develop your customer list through endless hours of research and phone calls and talking to people in your industry. It may even take years before you've ferreted out all the various trade shows, trade magazines, and industry organizations connected to your niche as the expert from out of town. You will be absorbing this vital information as you go. At the very beginning of your career, however, you've just got to start going for it. It's a grindstone, but it will pay off, and it's the only way to go nationwide.

You may call one trade organization, and be referred to another. This pattern may repeat itself until you've called ten and finally feel comfortable you've gotten to one that's close enough to the sort of outfit that serves the clients you're looking for. You purchase their mailing list, or perhaps you subscribe to their magazine, and start attending their conventions or trade shows.

This great nation of ours is so large, that even after ten years in printing, I still to this day happen upon new hunting grounds that suit my market to a tee. This past weekend I attended a trade show in Denver for the International Association of Facility and Venue Managers, the representative body for those who manage the major concert venues around the globe. PERRi Entertainment happens to do print jobs for a number of major venues, including Madison Square Garden. The IAFVM trade show revealed yet more prime targets of opportunity for me.

The point is this: the pockets of opportunity are out there. It may take years before you've discovered even the majority of them. Fortunately, all you need to really get rolling as the expert from of out of town is to locate one decent-sized pocket.

SOON WE'LL TALK ABOUT what resources are out there for you to use as you begin your detective work in developing your marketing strategy. But first, a reminder: you must remember as you begin your customer search is to concentrate on the national market. That means that you must avoid picking up your telephone book and scrolling through the Yellow Pages, or buying the membership list of your Chamber of Commerce, or finding out who sits on the board of trustees of your nearest university.

You are the expert from out of town. Your customer base exists outside your home area. Your legwork isn't going to involve the local market. Resist the instinct to wade into your marketing campaign by starting locally. You don't want to advertise in your area. You don't want to court the local press to let the world know what you're doing. Your hometown media doesn't reach your audience. Your audience is national, not local, so you need to think nationally.

Do not be cowed by this reality. Do not worry that you have bitten off more than you can chew. Do not think that the task that lies before you has increased exponentially because you are advertising yourself to the country instead of to the county.

You are not going to be assembling massive direct mailings to reach your prospective customers. The happy secret is that you will be finding your *nationwide networking zone*, and within that zone, you will be advertising to approximately the same number of direct customers you would were you a general service or goods provider in your home town. Instead of spending $500 to place an advertisement in your Chamber of Commerce's monthly newsletter, you're placing the same-sized ad, probably at the same price, in a trade publication that targets the sort of people you need to reach.

Yes, you're going nationwide, but you're not addressing the entire nation of 250 million souls. Rather, you're going nationwide in search of prime customer pockets, to cull from the enormous population of those individuals who fit the bill of your potential patrons. Think of it as a Zen-like approach: the market already exists; you just need to find it on your radar screen.

Recall the M.E.S.H. theory. You must expand ("E") your market nationwide, then sharpen ("S") in on the people who want your services. By so doing, you will likely end up with approximately the same number of potential clients you would were you local and unspecialized.

Were you a general contractor in Reno, someone who would build a fence as eagerly as you would build a house, you may have a potential market of 1,000 customers. As the expert from out of town who builds jails, however, you're looking for 1,000 specific customers around the nation who need to engage your expertise. That's the beauty of it. What would you rather target — 1,000 local mines, ranging from copper to salt to fuller's earth; or 1,000 gold mines? What would you rather be — a digger for hire, or a master geologist specializing in finding gold mines? Whom would you, as a customer, be attracted to more?

NOW WE'RE READY TO get down to the specifics of sharpening in and finding your pockets of opportunity. Where to begin? With publications. These include source books listing organizations and associations, trade magazines and newsletters. They include articles listed in the periodical indexes. They include membership rolls and mailing rosters.

The idea is to zero in on the trade magazines and newsletters that most closely target your market. You'll want to subscribe to these, and perhaps advertise in them. You'll also want to get hold of their subscriber mailing lists.

The same is true of organizations and associations. You'll want to identify which contain members that will be your customers. You'll want to join these groups or at least subscribe to their publications, and you'll likely want to get their mailing lists.

Your information-gathering process begins at the library. It's only a start, but it's a great place to start. Begin at the reference desk. You're going to look up the subject and industry you're in. One of my favorite resource books is the Encyclopedia of Associations and Organizations. Most libraries carry it. If yours doesn't, call the reference desk at another library. If the main branch of your public library doesn't have it, try the nearest college library, or try the library system in the nearest large city.

Remember Lorrie the travel agent who wants to specialize in touring entertainers? She'll leaf through the Encyclopedia of Associations and Organizations (or scroll through, depending on whether it's loaded into a computer bank), taking copious notes on the groups listed under such key words as "concerts," "tours," "bands," "travel," and so on. She may end up photocopying a dozen pages. Now she's divined what membership entities exist in the entertainment touring world.

Next, Lorrie asks for directories of periodicals. Newspapers and magazines are catalogued. The problem with these periodicals is they only list publications with reasonably large circulation. I can guarantee that the "Wizard of Oz" trade magazine I subscribe to didn't make it into these directories.

Yes, you may be amazed at the vast ocean of trade magazines out there. There are "trades" aimed at collectors of specific car models of specific years. I belong to a "Wizard of Oz" club, and it has a trade for "Wizard of Oz" fans. Its mailing list is perhaps composed of only 5,000 names. But if you're a designer of figurines, and decide to do a special line of "Dorothys," you'll be glad you put in the research hours that helped you uncover the existence of the "Wizard of Oz" trade publication.

Most specialty trades have mailings of about 1,000 to 5,000. That's good for you. You're honing in on precision targets. The figurine designer doesn't want a list of every doll-collector or fantasy fiction buff in the United States. The more narrow and specialized the audience, the better.

Lorrie ferrets the basic magazines on entertainers and touring. She takes down key information, including the numbers and addresses to order issues if her library doesn't subscribe to them and she can't find them. These magazines will help her network to her potential clients through articles and, especially, through the advertisements (normally in the back pages) listing services, associations, conventions, and other trade magazines and newsletters.

In this way, Lorrie sharpens her focus. She'll sharpen it even more by getting hold of the trade magazines and newsletters affiliated with her area of expertise. These, in turn, may list or carry advertisements for even smaller and more refined trade magazines and newsletters.

Lorrie should also get on the phone and call editors or reporters at the various trade magazines and newsletters for information on where to target her marketing campaign. Networking, networking, networking.

Here is a trick that works. Lorrie should tell each trade magazine and newsletter that she is considering buying ad space. This is a great way to get a couple free copies of the publication; you'll also be sent all kinds of information about the publication and its readership. That way you can determine whether it's an organization worth subscribing to, or, when the time comes, advertising in.

Here's one more benefit of scouring the trade magazines and newsletters. They may help you run across your competition, either in their articles or, more likely, their advertisements. It could be as small as a business card clipping somewhere in the magazine's back pages.

Should Lorrie come across a travel agent's business-card advertisement in a music trade, she should call as a customer and glean what she can. (Seem a tad unethical? Remember, you are in the initial stages of your career as the expert from out of town. Someday, when you're established and thriving, you can bet some other budding entrepreneur will be calling you.)

I should mention a few other resources at the library. Since you'll be spending a fair number of hours there, you might as well take advantage of them. You can leaf or scroll through the book subject indexes to see what titles relate to your area of expertise, on the off chance some valuable nugget of information can be turned up in their pages. Likewise, scan the magazine article indexes using key words defining your field. You may hit upon some interesting pieces that also yield solid bits of what detectives call "intel" — intelligence.

Finally, most libraries are on the Internet. We'll discuss surfing cyberspace in the subsequent chapter. I cannot express how important a marketing resource the

Internet can be for the expert from out of town. It will let you rapidly network with people who are listed on the 'Net by extremely refined subjects and interests. But again, that will be covered in Chapter Seven.

The problem with the library is you're probably not going to zero in on your exact niche. You're going to get your first feel of the big picture. You're going to begin to hone in on areas you'll be looking at. You'll have attained a vague outline of your treasure map. It will allow you to head home, get hold of the proper trade magazines and newsletters and work the phone for more information. All in all, it's a good first step.

NOW THAT YOU HAVE put in time at the library, and on the phone, and you have produced a file on the organizations and trade publications connected to your niche, you'll want to explore purchasing mailing lists from both.

Lorrie the stars' travel agent would be foolish to buy the subscription lists of the general circulation touring magazines, but the names of subscribers to the trade magazines and newsletters could prove a mother lode for developing her customer data base. The same is true of the mailing lists of clubs and associations.

Lorrie will first want to learn the size of each mailing list, and the cost. Some businesses sell mailing labels that are very difficult to photocopy, so the buyer must continually purchase new ones. That works for you, because it means the lists are continually updated. You won't be squandering money on direct-market mailers to people who have moved, dropped from sight, or died.

Lorrie, with several mailing lists of band management companies and big-name agents in hand, now has the seeds of compiling a direct-mail campaign with a thousand prime prospects. At this point, the incipient expert from out of town is ready to produce her first special marketing piece. There are some important elements to include in each piece. Fortunately, the very fact that you are the expert from out of town will help you.

Not long ago, I violated the rule of focusing solely on out-of-town customers and tried a little experiment. PERRi Entertainment did a marketing piece aimed at local businesses. It was beautiful. It was on 8 1/2 X 11 sheets on fine, heavy bond writing paper, mailed in large envelopes. The idea was to sell local advertising agencies on getting their color copying done using our new, high-tech direct imaging photocopier. I sent out 500 mailings. We did not get one response. Why? Because it was too general. Ad agencies receive marketing pieces from printers all the time, including those that offer color imaging. I had no leg up on the others. I wasn't any more qualified than them. I wasn't specialized.

Once again, this underscores the beauty about being the expert from out of town, for it is quite a different story for the pieces PERRi sends out to the touring industry. Out of 500 mailings, we'll typically field about 50 responses. We just mailed out a marketing piece to each franchise in the National Basketball Association and the National Hockey League. The piece described us as a specialty printer for the NBA and NHL, handling posters, passes, credentials, and other printing needs. We enjoyed a five percent response rate.

The success was due in large part because we were focused on these clients. In fact, each piece was addressed directly to a specific person with a specific title. Our mailers to the local advertisers had lacked this critical element. So the ad agencies didn't care about us.

But the NBA and NHL clubs noticed that we were from out of town. Therefore, they thought, we must be good. Why else would an out-of-town company be sending them information?

I must also point out that these clubs don't receive these sorts of mailers every day. They don't receive

packages from printers, much less the highly stylized ones
we sent out. So when they get such mail, they answer it.
(After all, they don't want to be left behind if every other
club in their league uses specialty printing!)

Most of all, though, I believe our success was
pegged to our having done our homework. We knew to
whom to address our mailers. We had called the leagues'
front offices and been faxed the names, titles and addresses
of the proper people to contact with each team. This is the
function provided you by your mailing lists.

Sometimes, such lists won't give the names of the
people to contact, just names of organizations and their
addresses. That's when you'll need to know what titles are
used by the industry you're targeting.   That's when
experience kicks in. The longer you're in your business, the
more buzz phrases and jargon you'll absorb about the
markets you're hitting. Remember the miserable time I had
at the beginning of my career as an expert, trying to connect
with the right people to buy my printing and graphics?
Remember how I wrote to record companies, entertainment
lawyers and the like? I finally learned that it's the "manager"
who makes such purchase decisions. In the world of stage
theater, however, it's the "company manager."

When Lorrie sends out her first mailer, she may lack
the names of the precise people who hire travel agents. So
she'll have to discover what the standard job title is. Perhaps
it's "agent" or "promoter," or "travel adviser." But she can
rest comfortable in one area: her marketing piece will be so
industry specific, so stylized, and sent from out of town,
that it will be something entertainment agents do not see
every day. They are likely to respond to it.

LET US NOW DISCUSS the elements of your first
marketing piece. We've already said it should be specifically
addressed to a person and/or organization. It must also be
something special.

Bill Harrah, the late gambling impresario who turned a storefront operation into Harrah's, a giant casino corporation, and in the process set the industry standard for class, knew the value of high rollers, the regular customers with deep pockets who loved preferential treatment. Harrah used to say he sent out "invitations that were too big to put in the trash can."

Your mailer, too, should be something too original to discard. Don't go sending a mundane cover letter on personalized stationery accompanied by your business card. If you're going to specialize in travel arrangements for touring entertainers, go to an advertising specialty company, buy a batch of little trinkets shaped like airplanes, and put them each in little boxes, sitting atop packets of airline peanuts. Don't confine your marketing piece to a cover letter. It has got to be unique.

Know this: letters are out. Letters are only for communicating, in lieu of a phone call or fax. They're not for selling. We're talking about advertising here. We're talking about marketing. Your "letter" could consist of a single sentence. It could be a white piece of paper with some gold print in the shape of a guard tower, with copy reading, "Glenn: the expert in jail project management. Fax 702-777-4444 for more information."

I call my marketing piece my "lead advertising piece," or "tickler." It's a small, interesting attention-grabber; and if they want more information from me, they'll respond. Your tickler should contain very brief and terse information: who you are, what you do, that you're an expert, and how the customer can receive more information. The vehicle for them receiving more information can be a full-color postcard that they handwrite their name on and mail back, or a slip of paper to be filled out and faxed back to you. Given our high-tech age, it could even be an e-mail address by which they can write you.

Were Lorrie to send out those tiny toy airplanes, each

could bear a little parachute with the message, "For more information . . ." followed by her fax number and/or e-mail address.

I sent the NBA and NHL teams samples of sporting products we'd printed, in a funky reply card that said: "If you want more information on the industry leader in printing and graphics for the NBA and NHL, fill out this card out and mail it back." Whatever your tickler is, it should be easy for them to send it back to you. If it's a postcard, it should already be addressed to you; and don't make them put their own stamp on it.

How to get the tickler done? You're going to have to invest some time and money. If you're not confident or enthusiastic about your own marketing concepts, it would be smart to go to an advertising agency for your first idea. The ad agencies will write your "copy," the words for your tickler, and help you conceptualize your campaign.

You can get much of the grunt work done yourself via desk-top publishing on your home computer or by going to a photocopy center. You'll be able to print out envelopes, stationery and response cards in a variety of colors. There are also companies such as Paper Direct that print letterheads, envelopes, fliers and brochures with generic patterns and backgrounds. You can order what you want for your desk-top publishing at home.

For the attention-grabbing doodad, you'll contact an advertising specialty company. This is a company who will make the fun little trinket for you, whether it's a pen, a little football, or, in our travel agent's case, a tiny airplane imprinted with the words, "Lorrie Haimes, travel agent."

If you can't afford the advertising specialty pieces, go with a little brochure or message; you can get it done at a Kinko's or similar full-scale photocopy center. Make sure it's colorful enough to not get lost in the mail shuffle. Make sure that the piece states at the top that you're an expert in your industry. Make sure the message is short and attention-grabbing enough that it's not something they're going to ignore.

Besides direct-mailing ticklers, there's another route you should consider at the beginning and down the road: a bag insert at a trade convention. Each conventioneer receives a goody bag. Trade shows generally charge from $150 to $350 to insert your item in the goody bags. A bag insert in a national trade show is a great marketing device, and you don't even have to attend the convention.

Finally, you should consider placing advertisements in one or several of the trade magazines or newsletters specific to your niche. Don't go crazy with this. You're still in the learning stages of how to reach your audience. It's better to get your toes wet at first. Which brings us to a concluding point about your first wave of marketing:

Check to see what works. I can't express how important this is. Don't go and send out 500 packages or a box full of bag inserts at conventions without a checkup system. Follow through!

Keep notes of where your responses come from. Keep a log. When you get a response, be sure to inquire how the person heard about you. Was it the mailer? Was it at the trade show? Was it a newsletter ad? Was it word of mouth? Do not expend your time and money and effort without finding out where your responses are coming from. This information will help determine your subsequent advertising campaigns for years to come.

When customers do respond to your ticklers, that's when you send them a brief cover letter and brochure explaining your business: what you provide, how you provide it, and your list of fees. Remember, the beauty of being the expert from out of town is that the fact the tickler is being sent from out of town will yield you a strong response.

AFTER YOU'VE GAINED YOUR first clients, it's

time to start hitting industry conventions, conferences, and trade shows. This means you'll be networking face-to-face. You'll be surprised at how many confabs are out there related to your field. As I said, even after ten years in my industry, I'm still coming across some I should have been attending all along.

I can almost guarantee that you'll attend a couple trade shows that you don't belong at. Don't be discouraged. At the beginning, you'll be attending various shows merely to find out what they're about, and to pass out business cards. Do not buy exhibition space without having attended a show first. Don't be in a hurry. This is not do-or-die. If a show fits you, next year you can rent a booth at it and display your wares. If not, cross it off your list.

Attending a trade show, conference or convention is not a vacation. It's all about networking. As such, you should treat it as work. You must not hide out in your hotel room or spend endless hours taking in the city's sights. Plan to rise at 6 a.m. and prepare to keep going until 11 p.m. All kinds of hospitality parties, breakfasts, coffee meetings, lectures, workshops, seminars, and demonstrations are on tap.

The shows offer ample opportunity to small-talk and exchange business cards. They'll reveal the lay of the land of your industry. You'll discover who the players are, what they do, what business possibilities present themselves. Equally important, you'll be becoming part of your industry's fabric. It may take you two or three years before you're a familiar face, greeted warmly by the "in" crowd at these affairs. At the beginning, you'll be sure to suffer from Teacher's Lounge Complex. You'll be intimidated at first, but only at first.

In the mid 1980s, I attended Performance Magazine's Annual Summit, in Palm Springs. I believe I talked to two people the entire time, I was so nervous! Nowadays, my networking is smooth and productive.

People are quick to introduce me to others. I do the same. I'm an insider now. Like any circle, it's difficult to break in at first at industry gatherings. People talk to those they recognize, and often those they have known for years. But persevere. Find out which events are for you, and keep going to them. Over time, people will get to know you. You'll start validifying your position in the industry.

The entertainment world will know that Lorrie handles the travel bookings for acts. She becomes a player. Over the years, as groups run through travel agents, they'll look around for new ones. They'll give Lorrie a call.

There is another tack to take at shows and conventions. Most organizers are eager to fill their slate of event speakers; there never seem to be enough bodies willing to serve as talking heads on panels or at roundtables. There's your chance! You need not be a practiced public speaker at this stage. Fortunately, serving as a conference panelist requires no refined elocution skills. You're not the only person up there. You're sitting at a table behind a microphone in a row with other experts. All that is required is that you speak about what you know when called upon or when an interjection is called for. Even if you answer only one question from the moderator, serving on a panel is a great way to get your face and name before the crowd.

How to get invited as a panelist? Write the organizers a letter beforehand volunteering your time. Most likely, they'll want to meet you first at the convention. They'll likely tell you that all spots are filled for this year. But after they've met you, they just may make room for you. Often, others fail to show up for panels and substitutes must be called upon. At the very least, hosts will try to get you on a panel for the following year.

In sum, industry involvement is very important. As you network in, and subscribe to specialized trade magazines and newsletters, and attend a few conventions, you'll find out which organizations and associations are worth joining.

You'll pay your dues and get on their mailing lists, which will keep you abreast of industry news, trends and upcoming events.

Being a member affords all kinds of privileges. Most organizations have insignia, and will let you reprint them on your business cards or letterhead. What's more, being a certified member instantly validifies your industry standing to your customers. It makes it that much easier, when you market yourself, for customers across the country to realize you are for real. Pretty soon, most of them will be hearing from you.

CHAPTER SEVEN
Creating the Illusion

As the expert from out of town, you are not just another entrepreneur, specialist, or consultant. Therefore, the image you cultivate for yourself distinguishes you from the rest of the pack. Everything about you — from your marketing material to your telephone and fax services — must speak to quality and professionalize you. It is all about creating and maintaining a façade, an illusion. The marketing and advertising techniques this chapter will discuss are specially designed to help you market your business nationwide. They are not general advertising techniques; they are not appropriate for the corner video store and other businesses in a local market. They are devices for reaching and impressing a national clientele.

It is important, particularly when you first start out, to appear to be bigger than you really are. It is of the utmost importance to carry yourself well. Image can be everything. A person respects a judge in a black robe; a judge in boxer shorts commands no respect. You must let your clients, who hail from far away, know that they are dealing with a tangible, viable company. If you don't look the part, you're going to lose their business. You might get clients to bite after receiving a marketing letter, but if they call and you can't field the call with the proper office support, or follow up with adequate literature or sample products, you're not going to come across as a professional, much less as the expert in your field.

I'm not saying you should lie about your size. I'm only saying that you should be proud of what you've got; hold your head high. It all really boils down to one

The perceived Expert.

word: professionalism. It means you must operate at a high level of competence, and that everything about you, from the way you dress and speak to the letterhead on your stationery, must be first-class.

WHEN I STARTED PERRi Entertainment Services Inc., I began with not much more than a fax number, and it wasn't even to my own fax machine. It was a fax number at a business down the street. I knew my trade, since I had apprenticed for another printer, and I knew my markets and customer profiles, since I had run a subsidiary for my previous employer, doing the printing PERRi was to do. The expertise was there, but the physical trappings for my business were humble, indeed.

I leased a tiny, 200-square-foot office and had the telephone company install a phone, but I couldn't even afford an extra $200 to buy my own fax machine. I was boot-strapping the entire project. I ended up locating a secretarial service down the street and rented the use of its fax number to include on my letterhead and correspondence. I'll never forget the day when Michael Ahern, a very respected tour manager, called. He was handling the solo tour for Keith Richards, the lead guitarist of the Rolling Stones. Ahern needed to fax me an art design to use on the backstage security passes. I held my breath as beads of sweat formed and began trickling down my face.

"Tony, I will fax you this art," Ahern said. "Stay on the line. It's coming through right now." Thinking quickly, I pretended another call was coming in, and I couldn't see the fax.

"Oh, wait, there it is," I said. "Let me take this call, I'll call you right back." Then I sprinted down the street to grab that fax. Close call.

Often in those days as a one-man shop, I would call-forward my office phone to my cellular phone as I ran errands to the bank or post office. I would answer my

The real Expert from out of Town™

cellular phone as if I were in my office. My theater background may have helped with this. Looking back, it all worked out pretty well. The point is this: if you don't have the cash at the start to buy every piece of equipment you'll need to maintain a professionally run business, with the proper luck and hustle you can still keep up the necessary appearances. Have confidence in yourself.

For more than two months I had to jog down the block from my tiny office whenever I wanted to get or send a fax. To this day, managers of such high-powered clients as Whitney Houston have yet to remove that rented fax number from their data bases. I still receive their communications at that location, though I'm proud to say that PERRi Entertainment now has three fax lines all its own.

Incidentally, one thing I never did was let my guard down. I would never have spilled the beans to Michael Ahern that I had to head out the door to receive his fax, any more than I would have confessed to Bobby Thrasher, Billy Joel's manager, about how pleased I was to have finally landed my first account. Those would have been fatal errors. Never, ever, compromise your image.

As a footnote, I should add that if Bobby Thrasher or Michael Ahern were to read this chapter today, I doubt very much that their attitude toward me would suddenly change to disdain. I trust that they would respect me as a strong enough person to have pushed my way up from the pavement through sheer doggedness. You *can* get the job done at the outset with good stamina and hard work and faith in yourself. Know this: in time, as clients come your way and your earnings increase, you will find yourself growing to fit your façade.

EQUALLY IMPORTANT TO THE willingness to project a professional appearance is the banner under which you are to operate. What's in a name? Plenty, as I've

learned. As I write this, PERRi Entertainment Services Inc.
is seriously contemplating undergoing a name-change. We
may substitute, "Entertainment Services Inc." with,
"Printing and Graphic Services," or jettison it altogether and
just go with "PERRi Inc."

When I first began PERRi Entertainment
Services Inc., I intended, as a lot of young entrepreneurs do,
to serve as a one-stop shop. As I will discuss in Chapter
Eight, it got me nowhere trying to wear an assortment of
hats in the entertainment industry, from printer and graphic
designer to even band manager. The name was partly to
blame, for I selected it for its generalness. Its description
allowed me to take on whatever business happened my way.
As a result, I lost focus and squandered precious time and
energy heading off in wildly divergent directions.

What you name your business is critical, for it
not only presents you to the world, but it forces you to focus
on what your business is truly about. Do not repeat my
error by coming up with a vague, catch-all, generic name.
There are two tracks you can take: make the name simple,
using a family name (e.g., PERRi Inc.); or use the name as a
description of what you do (e.g., PERRi Printing and
Graphic Services). Remember, your customer is the most
important person in the client-business relationship. The
client must not be left confused.

There have been hundreds, if not thousands, of
people whom I've handed my business card to at
conventions and trade shows. The card read, "PERRi
Entertainment Services Inc."   Had my business' name
informed them what I actually do, I would have made much
more immediate headway. Instead, I had to go the extra
yard by explaining to them what PERRi Entertainment
Services Inc. actually did. If you are going to opt for the
route of a simple name, such as PERRi, make sure your
business card contains a brief description of your business
under the name. Let the world know what you do.

YOU'LL NOTE THAT WHEN I came up with the name PERRi for my business, I gave it a couple of flourishes. One, I spelled it the Italian way, with an "i" rather than a "y," reflecting my ethnic heritage. Two, I made the first four letters upper-case. This was partly for its aesthetic appeal; but there was also an old advertising trick involved. Anytime a newspaper reporter, trade journalist, or other print scribe writes about us, we emphasize that our name is spelled with the first four letters in all-caps, P-E-R-R-, and the last letter in lower-case "i." This way, any time our name is reproduced in an article, it presents itself as our logotype, or "logo." In other words, as our advertising symbol.

In a newspaper story or trade write-up, "**PERRi**" stands out, calling attention to itself. Many of the greatest logos — **3M**, **McDonald's**, **AT&T** — are all in Helvetica-type font, a very common publication style. Whenever their names appear in print, they resemble their logos. This is one reason for doing this.

Along with selecting a name, you need to invest some brain power into coming up with a business logo. It provides instant recognition, whether it's the golden arches incorporated into the McDonald's logo, or the distinctive cursive type of *Coca-Cola*. If you're not a graphic artist, don't try to produce the logo all by yourself. Come up with some sketches, then find an advertising firm that will finish the logo for you. You shouldn't pay more than a few hundred dollars. Here are three tips for designing a proper logo:

• Make sure it will show up if it's printed on a photocopier machine. Reduce it as far as you can and then enlarge it as far as you can. See if it still appears distinctive. Does it still come across? If it does then it is a viable logo.

• See whether it presents itself well in black-and-white. Don't make the mistake of creating a logo that only looks good in the colors you've designed it in.

    • Finally, opt for simplicity of design. Avoid complex or intricate drawings. Remember the applications for which you will use the logo. You'll want to have it embroidered on T-shirts and caps, displayed on billboards, painted on your company's cars and trucks, adorned on the windows of your office, and included on all your printed goods: stationery, business cards, fax sheets. If your logo doesn't fax legibly, throw it out the door and find a better one.

    Logos and names alike serve not only to convey instant identity, but to psychologically lock customers in to the fact that yours is a business of substance and importance. The distant client will rarely see you face to face. Your name and logo will become part of you. The client sees your logo at the top of the envelope or fax and instantly connects it to you. A snappy name and logo take on a life of their own. They add substance to your image.

    Finally, you'll need to legally protect your name and logo. The simplest way to ensure a business name is to go down to your local courthouse and apply for a fictitious name. The clerk's office will search through records for anyone else in your state using the same name. If you're home-free, register the name. Incidentally, many people use their family names to avoid the chance of duplication.

    The least-expensive method to secure a logo while you are registering it is by the "poor man's copyright." Simply put your logo in a sealed envelope and mail it to yourself by U.S. registered mail. Don't open the envelope; store it in a safe place, such as a special file or safe deposit box. It can serve as admissible evidence in case of legal action.

    To gain extra protection and make sure you don't infringe on anyone else's name or logo, call your state bar association's referral service and find a lawyer who specializes in patent and copyright law. The lawyer can conduct a national duplication search and ensure that the proper legal forms are filed. (A lawyer can steer you clear of legal land mines, such as mistakenly using an © instead of a ™ or a ®.)

Along with a name and logo, you should also have a public relations ("PR") photograph taken of yourself. Have roughly ten 4 X 5 or 8 X 10-inch glossies made. Avoid offset prints (reproductions with little dots) because they don't reproduce well in newspapers. Many firms or clients will simply ask you for a personal photo in the course of initiating business with you. An easy method to get a nice PR photo done is to first hire a professional photographer. Ensure that your photo reproduces well on a black-and-white photocopier. If the highlights and shadows are well-defined in a photocopy, you can rest assured that the photo will look good in print, where low-quality photo reproductions are often used. Dress comfortably for your photo shoot. When you're at ease, you portray confidence.

NOW THAT YOU'VE TAKEN care of your name, logo, and PR photo, you need to consider the startup electronics for your office. You will need access to considerably more equipment than the telephone and electronic typewriter that would have let you get by 15 years ago. This is the Information Age, you can't operate an office these days without a computer. The computer will help you in four different ways: word processing (writing your correspondence and reports, and performing some record-keeping); graphics (you'll do some of your own fliers); calculating (spreadsheets); and communicating (via the Internet, which we'll discuss later in this chapter).

The most important consideration when buying the right word processing program can be summed up in two words: be compatible. Have equipment that allows you to send your discs to others who can easily access them. There is a very well-respected graphic designer I know who has

Be compatible.

always wanted to be on the cutting edge. PERRi's printing facility has an output service to help people print their graphics. This designer used our services, but he wasn't compatible. He had a Macintosh computer, but insisted on doing his storage on a high super-gigabyte optical drive because it was so much faster. The drive was the latest storage device on the market. The problem was, hardly anyone else was using it yet.

PERRi uses Syquest discs, one of the two industry standards. The other standard disc is Bernoulli. This designer didn't want to use either of these discs. Every time he brought his work to our office, he had to tear his computer down and bring over his own hard drive to be able to print out his graphics. It was such a comedy! In order for him to be "so cool" with his high-tech equipment, he had to spend five hours messing around with his system every time he needed a print-out. The result was wasted time for everyone. The moral: when you're selecting your computer equipment — whether it's the storage device, the printer, the hard drive, the software, or the discs — be compatible.

Even the dominant computer manufacturers, have programs and equipment that are compatible with each other. To be certain you're in sync with your industry, call around first and find out what others are using, then go with it. Those who aren't quite yet computer literate may consider conferring with a computer consultant to ensure they have everything they'll need for their computer systems. The basics include a word processor with an office package, such as Works, which will allow you a fax line via a telephone modem; enough memory on the hard drive to allow you to work quickly and efficiently; and a laser printer.

Of course, you'll need a telephone line for your office, by which you can not only make and take calls, but hook up your computer's fax and also tie into the Internet. Your telephone system is equally important. You must be able to receive calls at any time. The key is to make it as simple and aggravation-free as possible for your clients and suppliers. Try to avoid making them miserable with voice mail. No one likes the feeling of being at the mercy of a machine, which is not only dehumanizing, but leaves the nagging suspicion that one's message has dropped down a deep dark hole.

An answering machine, I've learned, is not the ticket to running a successful business. A real live human voice is required. Therefore, I subscribe to a doctor's exchange where the fee is $60 a month for X-number of phone calls, and every call above that total costs about 25 cents each. The service is extremely professional, and provides a live human voice 24 hours a day. This is vital for the expert from out of town, whose customers live in different time zones. In sum: your startup electronics don't require an inordinate investment. What is called for is intelligent planning that allows you to fit into the computer world and to send and receive telephone calls in a competent manner.

YOUR MARKETING PIECES AND other graphics, including fliers, letterhead, and business cards, must look professional. There is no margin for error or sloppiness anywhere in your undertaking, certainly not in the printed materials that are meant to sell you to the world. It would be like trying to attend a royal ball in a T-shirt and jeans. You must be first-class all the way. Unless you're a graphic designer with the right computer hardware and software to prepare your own marketing pieces, I recommend you check out a company called Paper Direct. This firm has stock fliers, marketing pieces, Rolodex cards, and other generic printed goods that you can buy in bulk and add your own black-and-white printing to.

Another method is to have an advertising agency design a format that you can work with. Your marketing piece, such as a full-color brochure, needs to tell people right away what you do. I throw away a lot of mail that doesn't get right to the point. The best type of marketing piece is what I explained before, the lead advertising piece or "tickler." Here's a recap of what a tickler is. It is a device to elicit customer responses, so you can accumulate names of serious prospects for your key mailing lists. You should have your ticklers ready to mail out in bulk.

This book is not a how-to course in writing or designing a marketing piece; other books are available for that. However, it will tell you that the general elements of a marketing piece include who you are, what you do, where you are, and why you're an expert. The quickest way to get a good marketing piece produced is to go to an advertising agency. Just be sure to let the agency know you're not a one-stop shop; you're a specialist. Let them go from there.

You should have several different marketing pieces — one for each wave of mailed advertising. Your first piece should be a brief, post card-sized letter introducing yourself. The second piece can be a full page-sized letter. The third piece could likely be a full-color, high-impact brochure going into a detailed description of your service. Its pages should feature your photo in addition to your name and logo, which are to be printed on all your graphics. Your business cards, which you carry with you to hand out as circumstances warrant, should say in as simple terms as possible what you do. Mine say, "Printing and graphics for the international touring business." I don't leave people hanging, I've learned.

My first card said only, "PERRi Entertainment Services Inc.," along with our phone and fax numbers and address. People used to look at me and say, "Well, what in the world is entertainment services?" I imagined someone heading home from a convention with a pocket full of business cards from assorted people, flipping through and gazing at mine, trying hard to remember who exactly I was and what business I was in. I couldn't blame a person for tossing my card away. It didn't indicate whether PERRi did printing, hired out jugglers, or provided ladies of the night.

Eventually my card evolved into a true marketing piece. Today, it is a folded card. Right on the front it says that PERRi is a printer and graphic designer. Lift up the flap, and inside is listed ten of our specialties, including "posters," "logos," "backstage passes," "tickets," and "programs." Our PO Box, 24-hour phone and fax numbers, e-mail address, and Internet website are listed at the bottom and are visible from the front since the flap doesn't extend all the way. The back of the card contains our mission statement.

LET'S TALK ABOUT "placed advertising," ads you'll pay to have appear in a trade magazine or newsletter. You must have a professional design them. There is nothing worse than scrimping on the cost of creating an advertisement when you'll be paying $500 to have an ad appear. Can you imagine schlocking up the ad by doing it yourself on your computer's desk-top publishing? Giving it a terrible border, standard fonts, generic graphics, and a poor quality photo, so that it looks abominable in print? This happens all the time, folks. If you pay for nothing else from advertising agencies, at least have them do your logo and your placed advertising. If they are done professionally, they will bring you clients. An agent will make sure you don't include an overly wordy or confusing ad, and that the copy carries punch. Agencies can make even a small, 2 X 2-inch ad sing, and the ad will look ten times better than if you attempted to create one yourself.

When you go to buy a placed ad, you may be pressured by the salesperson to "act now" because "the spots are going fast" and the deadline is almost passed. If this happens, hang up the phone and never call this person again (well, you might not need to be that harsh). Deadlines run like clockwork. There is always the next issue. Do not be 7bullied. I have been suckered into buying $2,000 ads by hard-sell hucksters. I will not tolerate this any more. A good publication always has plenty of advertising and doesn't resort to arm-twisting sales tactics.

When should you advertise? The short answer is, when you can afford to. The placed ads will be your best device for reaching a wide audience outside your home area. But the direct-mail marketing pieces, sent out to the names on the lists you've developed (as per Chapter Six), will get you started. Start off with the simple lead marketing piece that says generally (and as tersely as two lines) what you do. It should also include a phone, fax number, and/or a postal or e-mail address that allows the customer to contact you to get more information. Mine says: "If you want more information, fax this form or call us, and we'll get a catalog out to you."

Give customers something that allows them to respond for more information. A post card-sized, stamped response card can work. Make them feel like they're not committing to buy anything. You're not going for the sell right away. What you are after are leads. On the mailer refrain from including a little box which reads, "Yes, I'd like a salesperson to call me." That may guarantee a prospective customer won't call or write back. A simple, friendly, non-pressuring, "If you'd like more information or a catalog or samples . . ." note on a return mailer offers a win-win situation. If the recipient truly is a prospect for you, then he or she will respond, and you can take it from there.

Remember to be passive at first; your products or services will sell themselves. Let me reiterate that brevity should be the soul of your first lead advertising mailer. I have sent out lead pieces that were composed of nothing more than a picture of a poster I've done for a client, and the words: "Printing and graphics. If you'd like samples, call us." I also made sure that our address, phone, and fax numbers were included in an area of the ad apart from the response section, so that after they returned that section they would still know how to contact us.

I mail out marketing pieces several times a year. I've learned that consistency of format helps imprint a business on the minds of customers. Use the same stock and color of paper, and try to find something unique. I use a recycled, brown paper bag-type of paper. The paper alone identifies PERRi Entertainment to the recipient. Like the name and logo, it's instant identification.

YOU NEED NOT CONFINE your marketing pieces to mailers and placed ads. In fact, as time goes on, you shouldn't. There are other effective ways to grab the attention of prospective clients. One way is by publishing your own newsletter. Remember, you are creating an illusion. A single-page newsletter that arrives every two or three months lets your clients know you're thinking about them, and that you're on the cutting edge of your industry. You're coming up with new ideas and products all the time.

You're really with it.

The trick with the newsletter is to avoid sounding self-serving or self-aggrandizing. You don't want to talk about how great your company is and trumpet its successes. The newsletter is not to come across as a boastful advertisement, rather, its contents should provide information useful and interesting to the customer.

You need not have the newsletter produced by someone else. You can publish it yourself on your computer, with the right software. Plenty of newsletter programs now exist. There are even CD ROMs that contain thousands of short, general-interest articles on such topics as eating healthy or staying fit, and "words of wisdom"-type items that you can use as "fillers" to flesh out your pages.

My newsletter, which goes out three or four times a year, tells customers about new trends and technology available in printing, cost-saving methods, new products from PERRi, better ways to send us their computer files, and so on. "News they can use." The newsletter also lets them know that PERRi is actively researching its industry, trying to find better ways to produce products. If I happen to go to a trade show and come upon a new piece of equipment that PERRi ends up purchasing, I'll mention the equipment in the newsletter and explain how it will enhance our service abilities. I'll say something like, "The new product will be available within three short months."

If you have extra time, you can personalize some of your newsletter mailings by attaching little notes to customers you're already doing business with, drawing their attention to various items you believe will be helpful to them. Again, a newsletter drives home the point that your business is always looking out for its customers, trying to find better ways to serve them. It says you truly care about them.

Promotional items (advertising specialty pieces that bear your company's name, logo, and phone number) are another effective way to pump up your marketing.

Advertising specialty houses (check your Yellow Pages) offer an incredible assortment of trinkets and goodies, from pens to key chains to Frisbees to flashlights to towels that come in small blocks that expand to full size when soaked in a wash basin. How to choose the right promotional piece? The best way is to ask yourself what *you* like. Odds are that your personality and tastes mirror those of your clients. Go with your gut instinct. My only cautionary note is that you should avoid calendars. People don't need you to send them calendars because most have their own way of keeping track of dates and events. They are inundated with calendars from businesses. Send them one more calendar and it'll get tossed.

I must also stress that the promotional piece you settle on must be a quality product. Don't send out junk; that sends a negative message. Nice T-shirts, hats, and notepads have worked for PERRi. I have sent them out to potential customers. Regular customers, meanwhile, have received a more expensive class of promotional piece. You may wonder why we'd send out pricey presents to customers we're already doing business with. Our reasoning springs from market research that showed most of our business comes from referrals. Thus, we need to reward our customers who send us new clients. Remembering them "after the fact" is very important.

I once purchased a number of expensive flashlights to send to highly valued customers. I surprised the specialty company by saying I didn't want PERRi's name on the flashlights. I reasoned that the customers would always remember who sent them the flashlights, and would likely appreciate them if they didn't bear PERRi's name on them. Expensive promotional pieces are the exception to the rule of putting your name on everything you send out. They are the only exception.

ANOTHER WAY TO INDIRECTLY advertise

your business is to include your name somewhere on your finished products or services. PERRi is a printing service, so it's easy for us to include, in very small type, our name on the credentials, tickets, and posters that we produce. The next time you go to a restaurant, scan the menu and you'll likely find the printer's name on the spine, back, or bottom.

If you're preparing reports or proposals for clients, make sure that your name is included somewhere on the finished product. If you're designing uniforms, include a tag with your company's name. Designing a building? Cut a deal with the buyer beforehand that you get to place a plaque somewhere on the grounds that identifies you as the architect. Have you ever noticed that chain-link fences around large properties always seem to include a sign listing the fence company's name? There's no publicity like free publicity. Which brings us to the media.

Getting interviewed by trade magazines or newsletters can generate useful free advertising. These entities are always looking for subjects to write about. How do you submit yourself as a topic? Call them. Ask what it would take for you to get an article in. Very few reputable publications will charge you for the favor of featuring you in their pages. They're hungry for new topics. The longer you've been in business and the more successful you are, the better your chances are of getting a write-up. Have black-and-white photographs taken of you and your clients with finished projects or at industry events. Trade publications can use these photos with the articles they write about you. In fact, the availability of the photos may boost your odds of being featured.

Here's one more technique for garnering free publicity: canned writing. Write your own story (or have a professional writer do it), and submit it for an editor to easily drop into the pages. Don't concern yourself with landing stories in the local media. Once again, you're not local anymore. Your customer base isn't there. It won't hurt you to be written up in your hometown paper or interviewed by a local radio talk-show host, but why bother? It won't impress your clients. They're not interested in how you rate on a local level.

Radio and TV are the other two dominant media. Since you are only targeting a narrow niche of clientele in the national market, you won't reach them by appearing or advertising on shows geared to the general population. If, however, you can find some syndicated or cable show that is aimed at the sort of audience that largely includes your prospective clients, then you have found a valuable medium on which to get out your message.

I must say that production costs for taping high-quality radio or TV ads is very expensive. I doubt if they're worthwhile vehicles for you, but serving as an interview subject on an industry-related cable TV or talk radio show could prove valuable. Often, you'll know from your industry involvement what media shows relate to your field. Panelists at conferences often include broadcasters who have their own shows or columns. Without being pushy, you can let them know in a friendly way that if they're ever short of guests, you'd be happy to help them out.

NO DISCUSSION OF MARKETING or communication techniques is complete anymore without mention of the Information Superhighway. The Internet is already a prominent medium, and its importance is only going to increase exponentially up to and past the turn of the century. It is especially indispensable as a communication tool for the expert from out of town.

This book doesn't purport to be a primer on surfing the 'Net, but it will explain some of the basic information you will need to know in order to get started. A few essentials are necessary for the reader to grasp this modern medium. The Internet can best be described to the neophyte as a world-wide network of computers all linked up via phone lines allowing their users to communicate with each other. It is like a high-tech city.

The Internet is not country-specific. You can send messages in whatever language you choose. It is also not the property of anyone. No ruling body governs the Internet. It was designed by the Pentagon in the 1960s for government agencies to talk to each other during an event of a nuclear war. If one computer terminal somehow became incapacitated, it didn't affect the whole. That was the beauty of it. The Information Superhighway is like a vast spider web; if one tiny strand is damaged, the web still remains.

There are three major ways by which the expert from out of town can benefit from the Internet:

Communication. You can send "e-mail," electronic messages, to communicate with people instead of writing letters, making telephone calls, or sending faxes. This is not only hip, but quick, and rapidly becoming standard in the world of the late 1990s.

An Information Resource. The Internet serves as a vast and varied library by which you can access knowledge on almost anything, including highly technical tidbits for your own work. If you can't find the information anywhere else, you can send out a message asking other Internet users to help you out.

Marketing and Advertising. You can use the Internet to let people know about you.

The Internet used to be very difficult to access and use. The user would have to know computer programming, languages, and codes. Today, graphic interfaces have been incorporated to let the average person use the system with ease. The user clicks on the various icons to send commands. It couldn't be easier. All you need is a computer, a telephone line, a modem, and services from an Internet access provider.

I recommend three initial steps before connecting to the Internet. First, read up on it. You don't need to pore through one of the thick manuals available. One or two small books should serve the purpose of providing a reasonable orientation. Likewise, magazine articles in your public or university library's archives will provide good briefings. Secondly, attend Internet seminars. Like anything else, don't dive in without doing preliminary research. You'll need to understand what you're getting yourself into. Thirdly, go to your local computer store and find a Internet Service Providers (ISP). You will pay just as you pay the telephone company for using its phone lines. Double check available providers. Interview them. Find out what services they provide and at what rates. You may find that some are such techno-nerds that they're not for you and you won't want to deal with them. I interviewed five companies before I found one that I could communicate with. In short, do your preparation before heading up an on-ramp onto the Information Superhighway. Think of it as learning to drive and finding the right car before getting your license.

THERE ARE MULTIPLE WAYS to get connected to the Internet. I feel the best is to use a local provider, as described above. You will use your computer, via a phone modem, to call the provider whenever you want to get hooked up. This way you won't have to pay an hourly or by-the-minute service rate as you scan the 'Net for information, because you will only be billed for a local call. The local provider will charge you an initial startup fee, such as $30, plus a monthly connection fee, usually between $20 and $30.

If you're in a small community that lacks a local provider, you can still get on the 'Net. Their are many 800-

number-type companies poping up all over.

Another way to get "online" is through a commercial provider, such as America On-Line, "AOL," or Prodigy. You can subscribe to these. As I write this book AOL has become quite a player and seriously looking at better access to the World Wide Web.

AOL, Prodigy and local service providers can all serve you well. Spend some time researching all your options, one will be right for you. Each has a digital access link into the Internet. Via your telephone modem, your computer will talk to your provider, and the provider will, in turn, relay the signals to the Internet. Incidentally, I use my regular phone line when I'm on the Internet at home, even though it ties up the line more than it should. At the office, I use a separate line for the Internet.

LET'S LOOK MORE CLOSELY at the attractions of the Internet. E-mail will allow you to send memos and write letters to people who can in turn respond to you. Your e-mail address exists at your local provider's site, akin to a post-office box at the local post office. The address contains letters, numbers, and symbols. The first part of the address will indicate who you are (usually a nickname or abbreviation), followed by an @. The second part is where you are (your provider, such as AOL). The third part will indicate what your provider is, such as "com," indicating a commercial entity, or "edu," indicating an educational facility, usually a university. One of my e-mail numbers is *room501@aol.com*

If you ever need to look up prominent addresses, know that bookstores carry Internet directories, analogous to phone books, that alphabetically list sites and attractions. E-mail is not only quick (Internet users refer to the U.S. Postal Service as "snail mail"), but versatile. You can put attachments to notes you send. Were I, for example, to send my book publisher a message, I could include a photograph with it, using my computer graphics capability. You can also carbon copy (cc) your messages to ten addresses at the same time.

E-mail is more of a communication tool than a marketing tool. In fact, you should resist sending advertising messages cc'ed to multiple e-mail addresses. A minimum of such messages, done with taste, is passable; but continued practice is a violation of "netiquette." You will quickly become a nuisance. Also know that there is a method of retribution. It is called the "e-mail bomb." This is a practice where users begin dumping dozens or hundreds of messages into your e-mail box so that the important ones become buried. Appropriate ways to advertise on the Internet will be discussed later in this chapter.

"News groups" are another e-mail asset. They are sets of people interested in the same subjects, who discuss questions and offer answers. News groups allow you to find information on just about any topic. Let's say you're trying to ferret out facts about the best hotels in the West Indies. Find the right travel news group, and tips and opinions should begin appearing in your e-mail box.

"Chatting" is yet another communication attraction. It's just like a conference phone call. Send out a message to a chat group speaking on a specific subject, and anyone else can, and will, respond. Back and forth the messages go. It can be a useful fact-finding tool.

One more attraction is "FTP" — file transfer protocol. It is the process by which you can roam the Internet to "download," or retrieve applications, programs, and photographs. If, say, you want a new update for Windows, you can call the Microsoft station and fetch the program. Some of this is free; for some you are charged a fee.

THE MAIN TERRAIN OF the Internet is the World Wide Web. This is where you will do your advertising and marketing. The Web is devoted to information, and ads are accepted. It is also a fantastic tool for information-gathering. We'll talk about that first.

The Web is literally a network of hypertext. Hypertext links different websites to each other. With it, you can access newspaper and magazine articles, book synopses, encyclopedias, universities, and more. The list of such sites is nearly endless. You can browse for days on end and never be bored. The web is a freeway of endless visual graphics like billboards, from brochures to résumés to business cards. Let's say, as a hypothetical example, Cadillac creates a website. The website includes information on prices, mileage, photographs of the new line of cars, and other details. Prospective car buyers can access it at will.

As you scan the World Wide Web, you'll encounter groups of highlighted text (usually in blue) in sites that correspond, using hypertext, to still other sites. Merely by clicking your cursor on the text, it will automatically dial the site for you. It's that simple. So if, say, you're perusing the Cadillac site and you see a highlighted mention that Consumer Reports gave Cadillac a favorable rating among luxury cars, you can click on the highlighted section and the Cadillac page will close and you'll quickly be hooked up to the Consumer Reports page.

As a hypothetical example, I could look up the word "touring" on the 'Net, and find a Billboard magazine page. I'll call up that page and find the words, "Rolling Stones." I'll click on those words and get the Rolling Stones' web site. There, I may find the word, "Reeboks," because that company is sponsoring the band's tour. I'll click on Reeboks and find out all about its promotions. Thus, you can move from site to site very rapidly, gathering information as you go. That's what surfing the 'Net is all about. The World Wide Web is user friendly.

The second aspect of the Web is as a medium to utilize for advertising. You can do so in two main ways.

You can hire your local provider to create a web site for you. The provider will program it for you. Your site will exist in an appropriate sector of cyberspace. Let's say that Lorrie, our travel agent to touring entertainers, pays for a web site. She keeps it updated with travel information of interest to her clientele. To ensure that users will know where to find her site, Lorrie will try to have it hyper-linked from other sites related to the travel and entertainment industries. She can, as a hypothetical example, have her web site creator investigate whether she can have her site linked to the Billboard magazine page. Billboard may charge Lorrie a fee for this. The word "travel" will be highlighted on the page, and users who click on it will bring up Lorrie's web site page on which she features rates, methods of securing airline tickets and discounts, and hotels. The page will also include Lorrie's e-mail and postal addresses, telephone and fax numbers. The more web sites that Lorrie can link to, the more effective her advertising will be.

Netscape is a browser program by which users can browse the Web. Then there are search engines such as Yahoo were typing a key word (such as "travel") will bring up a list of sites that come under its category. Eventually, those most hungry for information on the sort of service that Lorrie provides will be able to find her website, also known as a "homepage." Having your own homepage is an investment, but it automatically validifies your standing as an expert from out of town. It is one more way by which you can bolster your façade.

You can also purchase placed ads on already existing web sites. Bill, our wood sculptor, could research which web sites are most frequented by aficionados of his art form, and buy ad space on those pages. He'll get a photograph taken of himself with one of his carvings, and place it — with information about himself, including his telephone number and address — as a paid ad on those pages. Web-site advertising will become to the entrepreneur what billboard advertising has been to big retailers. In a way it will even be more cost-effective. Each home-page advertisement will specifically target customers most interested in the goods or services featured. They will be a self-selecting audience, for they will have sought out the home pages themselves.

The Internet is the perfect tool to reach a niched market. What's more, as Internet access spreads to the mainstream, computer terminals are envisioned for copy centers, coffee houses, and countless other public areas. The Internet will join print, radio, and television as the fourth mass medium for the Global Village of the Information Age. Take advantage of it.

LET ME END THIS chapter by putting a twist to the old adage, "it takes money to make money." I maintain that you must be willing to invest money to make money. There are so many business people who hold themselves back, who require an immense personal effort to bring themselves to write a check. I admit I've made some mistakes in how I've spent money to build my business. I own equipment I don't use; I've hired employees who haven't worked out. Yet, all told, I've come out ahead. I've purchased technology that has proved indispensable to my operation. And out of every five employees I've had to let go, I've found that one ace in the hole who's allowed PERRi to forge ahead.

I am definitely the type who won't hesitate to whip out a check once I've become convinced the cause is worth it, but I believe I do so responsibly. I diligently track every single expenditure to see how it pans out. You, too, should not be afraid to spend money, and even to lose on a proposition from time to time. You'll never find customers if you don't advertise. Effective advertising costs money. Sometimes it takes trial and error before you discover the best ways to advertise, but effective advertising brings in business, and allows you to make money. From time to time, as your business grows and becomes better known, you may be asked to make a speech at a dinner or convention, donate to charity, host your own industry function, sponsor scholarships, and the like. Refrain from being stingy. Consider it exposure, and a way to build image.

In sum, don't be afraid to wager wisely to build your business. Invest in the proper marketing pieces and office equipment and telephone and Internet services. It will all work out for you. You will build up a potent enterprise with an impenetrable façade, and set yourself up to prosper as the expert from out of town.

CHAPTER EIGHT
Focus, Focus, Focus

In Chapter Seven, we talked about creating the illusion of a successful business (Not to say your business won't be). In this chapter we'll discuss how to make good on the illusion you've created. The most important task at hand at this juncture is to *stay focused!* Focus, focus, focus. This should become your mantra as you forge ahead as the expert from out of town.

You have found a niche for your specialized expertise and you are exploiting it by remaining tightly focused on what you do. You are a one-trick pony, and that's your strength, not your weakness. You may very well say to yourself, "Well, I know companies that do all kinds of things." Of course you do, but look at it this way: were you to go into a department store such as a Macy's, you wouldn't find different items mixed together in the same sections. Macy's isn't a three-story building where different colognes are found in every corner. Department stores focus: they put colognes and fragrances in one area, shoes in another area, lingerie in another. That's why they're called department stores.

Yes, there are businesses that wear more than one hat. It's because they've spun off separate departments, divisions or subsidiaries, each one self-contained and specializing in services or goods. As it stands at this moment, as you embark on your new enterprise, you are a single department, concentrating on the service you provide to a specific set of customers. There is a way to sharpen your focus, like twisting the lens control of a microscope. It is preparing what is called a mission statement.

ONE-TRICK PONY

A MISSION STATEMENT IS simply a sentence or two describing the work you do. It explains to your customers exactly what you are offering. It also has the advantage of reminding *you* of what you got into business to do. Your mission statement spells out precisely the *raison d'être* of your enterprise.

I've found that my mission statement is so central to keeping PERRi Entertainment Services Inc. on track, that it's worth actually printing on our business cards. The back of each of our folded cards now reads: *"OUR MISSION . . . is to provide the entertainment touring industry with quality and exciting graphic design and printing services, using the latest computer technology and traditional techniques, while providing a knowledgeable advantage, timely service and reasonable rates."* That may seem a bit long-winded, and indeed, I don't insist that the beginning expert from out of town craft such a lengthy statement. PERRi Entertainment Services Inc. evolved its statement over several years, but note that the statement doesn't veer off into tangents.

" . . . to provide the entertainment touring industry." That limits the scope of our market. We are tightly niched. *" . . . graphic design and printing services."* That's what we

do. " . . . *using the latest computer technology and traditional techniques.*" In other words, we're experienced but have up-to-date technology; *". . . while providing a knowledgeable advantage, timely service and reasonable rates.*" This is what is called "puffing." We're tooting our horn. Nothing wrong with that. We believe it.

A mission statement is somewhat akin to a New Year's resolution. The more specific you are, the more apt you are to be successful. A person who writes out, "I'm going to lose alot of weight" and seals it in an envelope on December 31 is not as likely to achieve his or her goal as the person who writes: "I'm going to eliminate fats and oils from my diet, especially fried foods, and I will go to aerobics class four times a week. I will lose 25 pounds by July." The defining difference is that the first person is unclear on how to go about achieving his or her goal. The second person lays out precisely how he or she will accomplish the goal, and the goal is very directly stated.

As you plan out your business in the initial stages, you should sit down and write out a short statement of what it is you intend to do. Glenn, our jail-builder, may fashion a mission statement along the lines of, "To provide the construction industry with expert consulting services and product management in the field of correctional facilities." Like PERRi Entertainment, he may add something like, ". . . giving projects the edge of experience, at reasonable rates."

Lorrie, the travel agent to the entertainment world, may create this sort of mission statement: "Handling all the travel needs of the entertainment touring industry, from ticketing to lodging to routing. Exploiting worldwide contacts with the full range of top-quality transportation and hotel services." A mission statement works rather like a mirror. Hold it up to yourself. Read what you're all about. It's what you're telling the world you are, and it's how your customers will read you.

ONE OF THE KEY benefits of writing a mission statement is that it helps you steer clear of the pitfall of over-extension. I wish I would have done a mission statement when I started PERRi Entertainment. It would have kept me from diverting time and energy into questionable side ventures and quixotic quests. At one point, I was smitten by the potential of a young rock band in Reno that wrote its own songs, looked good on stage, had a rather large local following, and seemed intent on getting somewhere.

I decided to co-manage the band, Midnight Sky, with one of my employees. I talked myself into the logic of the proposition: I had a ton of connections in the entertainment industry; surely an outgoing person such as myself could walk the walk and talk the talk. I could promote this band in the local market, building up a buzz that would carry it into the big time. As it turned out, I had neither the time nor the know-how to do it right. There I was, running a burgeoning printing business by day, and managing a band by night. That meant I had to moonlight, and my showing up was just part of the puzzle.

A manager has to be in charge of everything, from booking gigs at clubs, to collecting the band's share of the door and bar receipts, to loading up the equipment and making sure members have rides. Bands need guidance. They even need camp counselor-type intervention at times to smooth over relationships. Someone has to crack the whip and ensure they rehearse. Band management, to my chagrin, turned out to be a skilled occupation. There was also the matter of recording an album. This is the goal of every band. It, too, was a whole new world for me. Sure, I had the connections and the talent to manage a band, but I lacked the experience. I wasn't in any position to expend the blood, sweat, and tears to accumulate the necessary knowledge.

Thanks to the unceasing efforts of my fellow co-manager, Midnight Sky did record an album and was eventually able to have several thousand CD copies pressed, but in the long interim, the group stopped gigging, the buzz faded, our relationship dissolved, and the whole thing fell apart. Another band for the rock 'n' roll bone yard.

I'd be proud to tell you that my short history as a rock 'n' roll band manager taught me everything about staying focused on square one, but I'd be neglecting to mention the bookstore. What possessed me to buy it? My love for reading and books. The bookstore lasted one year. A lesson learned, again, about focusing and sticking with your niche as the expert from out of town. But did I mention the pretzel caper?

"The Knotty Baker Pretzel Company." (By the way, the name's still one of my trade marks, if anyone out there is getting ideas.) What got into me to make me try to capture the pretzel-eating crowd? Simple. I love pretzels. I also love the idea of the Hard Rock Cafes and similar themed fast-food eatery chains. I wanted my Knotty Baker Pretzel Company to be a string of beer-and-pretzel nightclub establishments. The waitresses would be dressed up like Betty Grable and the other women painted on those World War II B-17 warplanes. "Knotty" would serve as a double entendre to describe these beauties employed at my pretzel emporiums. I committed hundreds of hours over the course of six months researching this baby. I held business meetings, flew around the country to visit bakeries, even produced a pretzel in my kitchen at home. Yes, I tied myself in knots trying to make it work, and that's as far as it went.

It all got me nowhere. I ran out of steam and enthusiasm to execute my brilliant brainstorm. The disenchantment snapped me back to reality. My banker had told me that the least likely loan to secure is that for a restaurant. The reason is that more people open restaurants than any other business. They do so believing they know how to cook. However that doesn't add up to running a restaurant and most fail in the first year. When it came down to it, I knew how to throw a party and I knew how to make a good pretzel, but I didn't know how to put together and operate a restaurant. So I wasted a lot of time that I could have invested in my original company. Now, you've got to take risks in business. Otherwise, you'll never get anywhere, but my point is, take the risks within your own industry. That's where I'm taking mine now.

THE TEMPTATION AS YOU begin a new venture, and a temptation that will crop up periodically as your enterprise grows, is to grab whatever business shows up on your doorstep. It's the toughest thing in the world to let go of a client. A perfect example is what came my way not long ago. For the orders that require them, PERRi Entertainment does holograms, those three-dimensional images on photographic film that come to life when lighted. We did a custom hologram for the Rolling Stones of their famous Andy Warhol tongue logo, to go on the band's tickets, special invitations, and security passes. Alot of people in the entertainment industry, including the record industry, heard about our work.

Now holograms are now standard fixtures on everything from credit cards to the adhesive tabs that seal the wrapping on CD's. We got a call one day from a gentleman who sounded very professional. He said, "I've got 100,000 CD's that need the little tiny hologram pieces on them." He was offering us all this tremendous business. My sales person, Dave Paiva, looked at me and said, "I have this guy on the phone, he wants all these holographic stickers! Should we get into this?" I put the nix on it. Dave looked at me funny. "You want me to tell this guy to go somewhere else?"

As it happened, I knew of an outfit in the industry who makes just what the gentleman on the phone was looking for. I directed him to the outfit, DiskMakers. Holographic CD stickers are what DiskMakers produces.

It's what the company specializes in. DiskMakers manufactures CD's for the "indies," the small record companies, as opposed to the big corporate labels. Why should PERRi have gone and recreated the wheel? We don't make this particular product. We've never made this product. We would have had to learn how to do it and invested considerable resources in the endeavor.

As it turned out, by remaining true to ourselves the entire affair worked out very well for us. We ended up calling DiskMakers to ensure it got the referral. Now DiskMakers knows we're thinking of them. We're intertwining with another worthy company within our industry. We're also letting the gentleman with the 100,000 CD's recognize that PERRi is big enough to refuse business. I made sure my sales person let him know that PERRi Entertainment handles printing and graphics for the touring industry. We don't take on the recording industry. We don't produce CD jackets. We don't print cassette covers. We don't take on these huge accounts with runs of 200,000 to 300,000 at a time. We're a small specialty printer. We're the expert at what we do. Now the customer we directed elsewhere knows what we do, and he's going to call us someday when he needs us. That's the advantage of staying focused.

THE MORE YOU BECOME established as the expert from out of town, the more frequently you'll be approached by people with jobs that don't fall within your bailiwick. T-shirts are a hot item in the touring industry (as anyone who's attended a concert in the past 20 years knows). We are constantly plagued with customers calling us to make T-shirts for their tours. We decline. "Thank you very much for thinking about us. We are a printer. We are an off-set lithography house. We don't make T-shirts. Send your order to the T-shirt guy."

It's important to stay focused, for all the reasons

stated above. In fact, there are three additional, perhaps subtle, reasons to consider. For the first reason, allow me to harken back to a point from the previous chapter: staying focused will help build your façade. It will build your reputation and mystique. When people refuse business, they become invested with an enchanting quality. We don't give inquiries short shrift. We let everyone who calls us know what we do, how we do it, what we know best, and they respect us for that. We are not a one-stop shop.

Lorrie, our travel agent to the entertainment industry, doesn't like to book cruises. When clients of hers want to go on a cruise, she refers them to a cruise specialist. Lorrie meets a lot of very well-heeled, sophisticated people as she books travel arrangements for celebrities, so it is inevitable that she runs into clients who ask her to book their luxury travel safaris in Africa. Lorrie is smart. She graciously declines. She mentions a name or two of someone who might be able to help the client out. Someone who can make sure the client ends up in South Africa, not South America.

Likewise, Glenn our jail-builder doesn't hire himself out to consult on casinos or hotels or other projects. Were someone to approach him with praise for the way Glenn constructs correctional facilities and offer him the job of supervising the building of a shopping center, Glenn would do the professional thing and refer the person to someone with a good track record building shopping centers. Glenn anticipates the thinking of such prospective customers if her were to take the job. He knows they may wonder why he branched off to build a shopping center. Was it because his jail-building jobs had dried up? Glenn knows you're only as good as your last job. Which brings us to our second subtle reason to stay focused on your mission statement: You don't want to position yourself out of the niche you so carefully found.

A good example of this trap happened to a person we worked with on a David Bowie tour. This person was vastly experienced with managing rock 'n' roll concert tours. Well, this person decided to take a breather for a time in a corporate position, then ended up getting a job with the Nintendo World Championship. This was an event that traveled from town to town, staging tournaments for video game players.

The Nintendo gig was a tour in its own right, though hardly in the vein of the concert tours with which this person had built up his experience and reputation. After it ended, this person had a horrible awakening: he couldn't buy a job back on a rock tour. Try as he might, he simply couldn't blast back into the circle. As of this writing, he has yet to hook up with a band tour. He positioned himself right out of his industry. He had sabotaged his own referral list. Glenn is right: you're only as good as your last job, folks. Make sure that job is in your niche.

Now for the third additional reason why it's important to hold tight to your mission statement. Grabbing business outside your area of expertise can boomerang in truly ugly fashion. What if PERRi had taken on the job of printing 100,000 hologram stickers — and botched it? We could have ruined our good name in the industry. More frightening: we could have blundered into a large and unrecoupable business loss. Clients aren't charities. They don't pay on dead horses. We would have "eaten" the job. If someone sends 2,500 T-shirts to be printed and, because you don't specialize in T-shirts, you print them wrong and absorb the loss, it wasn't worth veering off into unknown territory.

Business jobs that don't jibe with your mission statement are bound to come your way. The question you're sure to ask yourself is: "How much money could I make?" "How much money could you lose?" is a more intelligent consideration. If you're dealing with a $100,000 job and goof it up, you could completely crumble your company. I'm not advising you to cavalierly turn away business; just to be smart.

Here's a simple exercise that may help you through the decision-making process:

1) Write down how much you believe you can make on the job.

2) Write down the worst-case scenario of how much you can lose.

If you take into account the latter consideration, you might be surprised how taking on the new venture could actually ruin you, that the "golden" chance is really just fool's gold. The risks outweigh the potential gains. Staying focused, on the other hand, involves no risk, only opportunity.

NEVER TAKE FOR GRANTED how much knowledge and experience you've accumulated in your area of expertise. You have paid your dues, you have learned the ropes, you have carefully accumulated sources and built connections, and so you can legitimately call yourself the expert from out of town. Within this realm you've created for yourself, you reign supreme.

I don't know a lot about textile printing. That is, I'm no practiced hand at the business of printing T-shirts, jackets, or hats. I field requests all the time to do this sort of work. I'm well-connected within the printing industry, but I don't fancy myself a printer of T-shirts. Likewise, I don't know a lot about CD manufacturing and producing jackets for these discs. Granted, I'm competent enough as a printer to study and learn such a specialty, but it would be a terrible thing if I bit off more than I could chew — or something I wasn't used to chewing — simply out of greed. Again, I would run the unreasonable risk of botching a job and losing money. I would lose a customer, damage my reputation, not to mention waste time that could be used to court or handle my regular business, my bread-and-butter.

It would be crazy for a brain surgeon to moonlight as a psychiatrist (both, after all, are physicians who work on the mind) merely for the lure of trying something new and potentially lucrative. That said, I must point out that it's OK to change your mission statement over time, but do so intelligently. Let it evolve naturally from your field of expertise. You need to grow in the right direction, not in the wrong direction.

PERRi Entertainment has begun to expand into the sporting industry. We are going to branch out to form a new division and give it a separate mission. The 1995 Super Bowl champion San Francisco 49ers have become a client of ours for special credentials and parking passes. This has opened up a whole new exclusive niche for our work. Having handled the tickets, posters, security credentials, and other printing and graphics for the touring industry, we're well-positioned to sprout into new industries. We've even handled elaborate security credentials for the United Nations. These are not missteps. This work is well within our area. The growth pattern is correct. We have the equipment and the know-how to get such jobs done perfectly. There is never any question.

Let us conclude this chapter by reiterating that if you don't know the business you're getting into, you're probably setting yourself up for a real stumble. We talked in Chapter Three about merging your passion with your knowledge. I like books, I like pretzels, I like rock 'n' roll, but that didn't lead me to success as a seller of books, a purveyor of pretzels, or a manager of bands. My knowledge is printing and graphics. It is a lesson I learned three times over the hard way. Hopefully, it is one I won't have to learn ever again.

I will say this: my financial advisers told me they wish they had learned at my age what I've learned. Indeed, these rather astute money mavens were past the age of 50 before they quit investing in businesses they knew nothing about. I've said this before but it is worth repeating: be highly specialized and tightly focused. Establish a niche and stick with what you know. You will prosper by it. Focus, focus, focus.

CHAPTER NINE
The Color of Money

It's the bottom line. The reason you're in business. You're a professional at what you do, not an amateur enthusiast. To make money, to earn a living, to put food on the table, that's the whole ball game. It means that every expert from out of town must be not only the authority in his or her field, but a hard-nosed businessperson, as well.

Yet, as anyone who has run a business for any serious length of time knows, there is such a thing as a client's bad debt. There is such a thing as having your electricity turned off if your payments are late once too often. Managing your cash flow is as vital as the marketing campaign that generates the income.

This chapter will address both ends of the money chute: how to ensure you get paid for the work you do, and how to pay your suppliers and creditors to ensure you stay in business. That said, there are four basic rules of conduct you should never waver from. For there is also such a thing as slaying the goose that lays the golden eggs. In your quest to bring in business and build up your bank balance, you shouldn't place your entire enterprise in jeopardy by developing a reputation for being a penny-pinching piker, or a human vacuum cleaner sucking up every dollar due past deadline, or an overly-busy bee that can't offer personalized attention to each and every client. In short, don't be short-sighted. You aim to be in business for many, many years, and with the proper professional attitude, you will be.

Rule No. 1 Is to never be blinded by greed. As we explained in the previous chapter, the expert from out of town prospers by staying focused. This means you'll inevitably turn away some opportunities that come knocking on your door because they don't adequately square with the services you provide. As I mentioned in Chapter Eight, PERRi Entertainment produces a wide range of printing and graphics for the international touring industry — but we don't do T-shirts. We stay away from textiles. It's not our thing.

There are times, however, when we will also turn away business that legitimately falls within our sphere. This is because we are booked-up with pending accounts. We have deadlines to meet, and it wouldn't be fair to either client to take on more than we can handle at one time. Please remember: a reputation is a priceless thing, and it is a fragile thing. You're only as good as your latest project. Mess up or do only a mediocre job — even once — and the word will get out about you. Make no mistake about it.

Sometimes, during peak season when my crew is hectically processing jobs, I practice an old trick. (I recommend this only by adding the caveat that you should carefully analyze employing this trick before implementing it.) It is equivalent to telling clients who call to "please take a number." I'll provide them a form to fill out with information on their project, saying once it's returned we'll analyze the form and let them know immediately if we are interested in taking the project on.

There are several positive effects to the "take a number" trick. One is that it buys you time to complete projects already in hand before taking on additional serious clients. Another is that the tactic can act as a lure. "Wow," the customer thinks, "I've even got to be accepted before I can give this guy my business." There is even a more subtle facet to turning down jobs, and it brings us to **Rule No. 2**: an expert always has work.

This gets back to the issue of façade that we discussed in Chapter Seven. Appear too hungry to take on work, and you'll not only lose your negotiating edge, but the respect of potential clients. The scent of desperation will be upon you. It is an unmistakable stench, and it scares customers away. In contrast, a person flush with business unfailingly attracts more clients to him or her, by virtue of being popular. "You can't get to me until the 15th of next month?" the customer asks. "All right. Let's work something out. I suppose I can wait until then, because I hear you're the best around."

An additional ramification of the attitude that you always have work is that you are never pushy in drumming up new business. Don't go wild with new marketing campaigns that promise great deals if customers *act right now*. Don't apply pressure tactics like the car salesman who uses the old ploy: "This price is only good tonight. Come back tomorrow and try to talk me down again, and you can forget it." The car salesman is a hustler to the masses. You're a specialist with a distinct clientele.

I have never been a "salesman." Because of this, I have inadvertently managed to entice or enchant some clients because I have never pushed my products on them. Instead, I am very confident in what I do. If they need me, if they want the best, they'll come to me. Repeat business has come to constitute 90 percent of my accounts. I have ended up with many clients who just like to tell me what they want and quickly get off the phone, confident in the knowledge they'll be receiving what they ordered. There is another side to this, though. You don't want to look too busy. There's a difference between doing well with a thriving enterprise, and being too good to take on the little guy. The proper stance to strike is one in which you're humming right along, but you're not above responding appreciatively to any legitimate customer who shows up. You're really on the ball.

Recently, a representative of the H.O.R.D.E. tour, an alternative rock concert series modeled after the successful Lollapalooza traveling festival, phoned. I was very busy when I received the call, and neglected to emphasize how very interested I was in the account. Subsequently, I lost the deal to another company that came across as more eager. Then again, that's my only such case of a lost account in a three-year span, or 2,000 jobs. In the grand scheme of things, I have won more clients than I have lost by being cool, not overbearing.

Another point I would like to make is that you must certainly never cut your rates in half because it seems like a lean year. Your rates are supposed to rise with inflation, not recede in desperation. An expert never panics. Which brings us to **Rule No. 3**: An expert is never hard-up for cash. That means the expert is never so hot to collect on a delinquent payment that he or she turns into the second coming of the Repo Man. Threats are for loan sharks. While this absolutely doesn't mean you're to be a patsy for flakes and rip-off artists, you're also not to devote too high a percentage of your precious time and strength toward collecting from those who can't or won't pay up, even for the "principle of the matter." You can't argue principles with the unprincipled. It's a lost cause, a dead issue. Which takes us right into **Rule No. 4**: situate yourself among good people.

There are more honest souls than dishonest ones in this world, newspaper headlines notwithstanding. The odds are nearly 100 percent that the unscrupulous won't be able to conceal their bad standings within the small sphere of activity in which you operate. "Burn me once, shame on you; burn me twice, shame on me," the folk saying goes. Burn enough people often enough, and the shyster, the crook, the thief all end up permanent members in bad standing with everyone connected to their field, blackballed for life. Which is the way it should be.

The expert from out of town nurtures relationships with suppliers and customers, quickly learning to ferret out those who aren't completely up-front, who equivocate, who don't keep their word, who come up with excuses and ridiculous demands and then question why there seems to be a lack of trust in the relationship. People who prove problematic, either in their unreliability or by difficult attitudes, are nothing better than energy drains, and ultimately not worth doing business with. Fortunately, they're in the minority in the business world. They're not built to last, you are. So surround yourself with the honest, upstanding, successful set. The winners, the good eggs. People just like you.

ONCE YOU'VE DEVELOPED THE proper frame of mind for practicing business, you need to begin exercising sound business etiquette. This is especially important for you, because the expert from out of town operates in a terrain different from the local business-owner. That is, the ease of doing business is complicated by sheer geography. Unlike the local entrepreneur, you can't very easily go to lunch with each and every supplier and get to know them. So it's going to be very hard to discuss buying inventory and services from vendors and suppliers, and to set up accounts on a faraway basis. Likewise, it will be very difficult for the expert to "knock on the doors" of every patron while collecting bills. That's why organization and discipline is so crucial to succeeding as a national specialist.

As we mentioned at the beginning of this chapter, there are two sectors of money management: getting paid, and paying up. We'll deal with the former first.

There are four general ways to bill clients, and each way reflects a different category of trust. 1. Long-term, faithful clients can be put on the "net 30 days" billing cycle, meaning your invoice is submitted to be remitted by their payment office 30 days after shipment. 2. The next-highest category of trust is the "net ten days" cycle, meaning you expect payment ten days after filling an order. 3. A common way to bill first-time clients or those deemed payment risks is "C.O.D." or cash on delivery. United Parcel Service,

Federal Express and other services deliver packages C.O.D., they collect payments from recipients in the form of cash, cashier's, or company checks and will mail them to you. 4. Finally, there is the "money up front" method, often characterized by a partial payment analogous to the retainer that a lawyer charges. This is often done in conjunction with a C.O.D., which is used to collect the balance of payment.

The beginning specialist may feel a bit uncomfortable about asking for a pre-payment or even a C.O.D., but consider this: when you go to buy tires for your car, you don't wait until the tires are selected, put on, and balanced and then try to negotiate to pay your local dealer after 30, 60, or 90 days. You'd be lucky to have your car returned with the old tires replaced, and told never to return! Your guiding light should be this: customers who intend to pay will pay for goods or services when rendered. You don't need to bother with the rest, for the most part.

What about credit? Many business people subscribe to the philosophy that they should be flexible enough to handle any client. That you need to take projects on to start generating revenue; and that sometimes this requires extending credit on demand. Hogwash, I say. What will invariably happen is you'll have trouble getting paid by the credit-seeker.

There have been very few times when I've run into people who've told me, point blank, "Unless you give me credit, I'm not doing business with you." In retrospect, their bluntness proved a blessing in disguise. For it gave me an easy out to decline their work. It's a terrible feeling hanging up the phone after telling a client you won't give them credit, while thinking to yourself, "I've just lost this big account." But remember, you're not a bank. The time you spend collecting on accounts of those who demand credit up-front is time you could spend productively elsewhere. This really all gets back to Rule No. 4 above: situate yourself around good people. Avoid "toxic" people like the poison they are. Customers who intend to pay will pay for goods or services when rendered. The rest you can send away as a "gift" to your competitors.

AS WE DISCUSS WHICH customers to put on which payment schedule, we need to look at certain techniques of how not to get burned.

No. 1: have a printed list of your terms. This aids your salesperson (which may very well be yourself when you start out) so that your customer doesn't try to finagle or change the terms either before or after the transaction. Restaurants have menus; stores have price tags. You have your printed terms. End of discussion.

Printed terms show you're professional, you've thought out your prices, you've settled on them because you believe they're fair. PERRi Entertainment's terms are printed on the backs of our catalogs, as well as on FAXable or mailable sheets of paper for ready distribution:

• Non-printed goods, such as bead chains for holding credentials, do not require deposits. We'll ship them C.O.D.

If something funny happens and the job is not picked up COD, we can retrieve the non-printed goods and put them back in stock.

• All new accounts must pay a 50 percent deposit with the balance paid C.O.D.

Even with those who pass our initial credit check, we still want 50 percent down. The rationale is that we need to cover some of our costs in case we don't get paid later. The customer has yet to establish a track record with us. (On the other hand, should they quickly pay the 50 percent, we will usually put them on "net ten days.")

• Customized goods (those made specifically for

the client) **require 50 percent down.**

• **We accept original purchase orders from universities, governmental organizations, and major corporations.**

• **Upon approval of credit checks, we extend to open accounts "net ten days" schedules, however we still require 50 percent down.**

• **We accept MasterCard, Visa and American Express**

Rule No. 2 for not getting burned: make customers fill out credit applications. Don't fill out the forms for them, as a car salesman does because he's in such a darn hurry to get you to sign on the bottom line, figuring he has but one shot at you. By making customers fill out the credit paperwork, you allow them to demonstrate they're serious about doing business with you. Sometimes we'll even accept people's credit ratings if it's for a smaller job — say, under $500 — merely on the face of how they're doing business with us: that they've filled out the forms, that they've behaved professionally and conscientiously and provided whatever information we've requested from them.

Just about every office supply store has blank credit applications for you to buy and use for customers. You'll use the information they provide to run a credit check, to ensure they'll be able to pay you for the work. PERRi Entertainment scrutinizes how professional and thorough a credit application is filled out. If it passes muster, we'll often not even pursue the process by calling a credit-check agency, such as Dun & Bradstreet. For larger projects, we do contact credit-check agencies. Customers who pass this test can qualify for our "net ten day courtesy billings." I rubber-stamp my billing envelopes with, "net ten day courtesy billing" to ensure prompt payment. Many companies have payment departments that operate on net 30 schedules, only cutting checks once a month. If they receive an invoice that doesn't say, "net ten" anywhere, it will get stuck in the net 30 cycle and you won't see the check until the next month.

As with the blank credit applications, office supply stores can provide you with general billing forms. I also recommend, "The Complete Handbook for the Entrepreneur," by Gary Brenner, Joel Ewan, and Henry Custer, published by Prentice Hall. The book contains many samples of forms and explains methods of handling billings, payments, and taxes.   I must also say that computer software programs are available to help you with your billing and bookkeeping needs, with forms to print out on your laser printer.

Rule No. 3 for not getting burned: folks who don't want to pay up front most likely will not pay. I've run into this time and time again: if there's a problem at the very beginning — if a client wants credit and doesn't want to put forth a dime up front — this means the client will usually never pay. There's a reason, after all, why he or she doesn't want to pay up front, no matter what the story is.   I've heard plenty of stories, and I've even been taken in by one or two. The most common features a line like this: "I'm bringing you more business. This is only a small job, but I've got much bigger jobs next year." That's a major red flag. I'll think, "Well, I don't care what you're going to do 'next year.' Why don't you want to pay me for this one?" Most people who promise you bigger, better action later on are not to be trusted. They are dangling forward a vision as bait because they don't have anything of substance to fish with.

Reluctance to pay at the start is a warning sign that tells you not to do business with the person. Again, this gets us back to the 4th rule of basic conduct: surround yourself with good people. I have harped on this several times already in this chapter, but it is vital you take it to heart. Reject big talkers before you get involved with them. Don't, and you're in for nothing but aggravation, frustration, and wasted work.

Rule No. 4 for not getting burned: if you're involved in an on-going project —say, supplying tickets and programs to a 50-stop tour — you can institute what I call "progress payments." Don't wait until the very end when all the work is done to receive one lump sum. Make it pay-as-you-go, on a net ten. If the payments begin to fall behind, then you can put the customer on C.O.D.

Rule No. 5: position yourself out of the billing loop with your client. This is another way of saying, let someone else do your billing for you. Pretend you're not in charge of that department. When I first went into business, I would have a friend make my billing calls. Remember the façade element. Yours is a sizable enterprise and you're too busy to wear all the hats. John buddies up with his client, Harry, forming the relationship at the beginning; then Betty the bookkeeper hounds Harry for the money. She's the bad guy, not John. If Harry gets wound up and calls John, John apologizes and says, "Hey, I'm sorry, it's totally out of my hands, the billing folks can be sort of persistent some times." Thus, John preserves his relationship with Harry. Another really good trick is to separate the relationship from the money yet another degree, by having your billing department deal with the customer's paying department. Then both of you are out of the loop.

Rule No. 6: C.O.D. not only lets you get paid faster, it builds your mystique. Not long ago, PERRi Entertainment finished printing the security credentials for the United Nations' 50th anniversary celebration. The U.N., as one might suspect, is a giant bureaucracy. We said up front we needed 50 percent down. We were very firm about our policy. It took a little convincing, but the U.N.

officials assented to the contract terms, including that payment of the balance would be C.O.D. Needless to say, the U.N. wasn't used to working this way, but we weren't prepared to hold out for 90 days until our bill was processed through the organization's labyrinthine internal channels.

Remember: you're the expert from out of town. You're able to use this to your benefit. Don't think of your insistence on C.O.D. shipments to collect the balance of a payment as a message that you're hungry for immediate cash. Think of it as a sign of status: you're big enough to require a C.O.D. deal. If young PERRi Entertainment in Reno, Nevada, can command this arrangement from the United Nations, then I believe any expert from out of town can do the same with his or her clients, whatever their prestige.

CERTAIN LARGE INSTITUTIONS present a different profile for getting paid. I am speaking of universities, governmental entities, and major corporations. Sometimes there's no avoiding the tedious machinations of large, unwieldy bureaucracies. If you refer back to PERRi Entertainment's printed terms earlier in this chapter, you will notice one saying, "We accept original purchase orders" from these organizations. That's how they approve payments, with purchase orders. It's worthwhile working with them because they are always good for the money. When the check arrives, it won't act like it's made of rubber. It's just that it can take a long time to get paid.

City, county, and state governments, federal agencies, colleges, and major corporations — they all have myriad departments and desk jockeys across whose fiefdoms your purchase order will cross. The university in Reno, recently appointed a "Red Tape Committee" to trim such unwieldy paper trails as a 32-step approval policy for processing a grant application. In some cases, the research that the grants are going to fund is completed by the time the grants are finally given the university's seal of approval. The committee itself took a year to come up with a final advisory plan to submit to university officials. The trick to getting paid by these institutions is to get the actual, original purchase order for your work. Record companies have what they call "purchase requests," "requisition orders" and "purchase orders." Don't mistake an approval to purchase something with the actual document granting that purchase. "Send me the original purchase order," is your line.

It is also important, at the very beginning, to itemize every single cent of your projected costs, including such expenses as travel and shipping. All those expenses should be contained in the purchase order's total. Large institutions run on budgets. They may come back after your invoice has been submitted and say something like, "We agreed to the contract for $30,000, but we're going to argue your expenses, your shipping, your taxi fares, you're handling fees and your custom fees." They'll pay the fee agreed upon, but not added costs that weren't discussed. Therefore, your expenses must be agreed to in writing beforehand. Make sure they are.

Another smart move at the beginning is to ask the person you're dealing with for the name of the contact person in the accounts payable department. Introduce yourself to this person when you're starting the job. The person's attitude will clue you in right away as to whether you'll get paid in a timely fashion, or if the whole affair is going to develop into a problem child. Most of all, though, you should feel secure dealing with the behemoths. It may take a bit of time for your check to grind through their giant bodies, but it's a safe bet that you'll get your money. Of course, if it's a one-shot job, not an on-going business relationship, you can insist on C.O.D., the way PERRi did with the United Nations. Whatever you do, please don't accept a purchase order from a large institution for a small order of $200 or so. Send the work C.O.D. The institute can handle it.

PROBLEMATIC CUSTOMERS PRESENT a whole different profile for getting paid. With skill, luck, and experience you will suffer few of these accounts in the course of your career, but at least a few will disgrace your path. The first thing to do is to consider how long the customer has been with you. If it's been a ten-year relationship and this is the first time he's ever gone ballistic on you, analyze what the problem is, then take good care of him. You don't want to lose him. But if it's a first-time customer and already crises are developing, let him loose right away. If it's the first time you've ever touched the client and he's already giving you problems — "see ya." You've got more important work to do. Let the competition have 'im.

Problematic customers have attitudes. They don't treat you very nice. They believe it's an honor for you to do business with them. They're toxic. You'll get much farther without them. Occasionally, a longer-term client will turn on you and you'll have to break relations.

The Rock 'N' Roll Hall of Fame, before it occupied a permanent building in Cleveland, was for years a going concern inducting acts at yearly ceremonies broadcast on live television. PERRi handled the printing for these events. For many years, the show was held in the same facility. One year, the venue changed. Unfortunately, no one at the Rock 'N' Roll Hall of Fame bothered to inform us. All of the printing we sent out listed the wrong venue. With 200 separate jobs going at a time, PERRi has no opportunity to play mind-reader with each individual client. What's more, we had signed proofs from the Hall of Fame's personnel who were supposed to have scrutinized the work to ensure it was completely accurate. They had signed off on it, we had printed the product and shipped it.

Had the miscue been our fault, we would have

readily accepted responsibility and rectified the error at our own expense. We've done that in the past. Yet this clearly was a case of miscommunication that originated from the client's side. It was blatant stupidity. We literally had proof, yet, we offered a compromise. If the Hall of Fame would at least cover the costs on the rerun, we'd put in the hours to print out product bearing the proper venue. The Hall of Fame's people blew up at us. Before they finally agreed. We shipped the rerun C.O.D. They paid with a company check. . . . And promptly stopped payment!

This taught us a lesson. When shipping C.O.D. to a problematic customer, do so with the requirement that payment be cash or a cashier's check. It's your option. And it's how you ensure you won't get stiffed. For the most part, our experience with the Hall of Fame was an extreme example of a relationship gone sour. Most of the time, when a dispute arises, it's partially the fault of both sides. The best policy is to keep it cool until the check clears. If there are problems, there's no reason to inflate the problems by sabotaging your chances of salvaging the business relationship or at least of getting paid. Don't yell at your customers. Don't start feuds. In my industry, there are a tremendous number of big egos. Sometimes it's nearly impossible to make certain ones happy. I remember one singer who hated the color purple — how could we have known?! — and rejected the printing job we'd done. We had to redo it in a shade of blue to his liking. The point is, there will be times when you just can't win.

There's one trick that certain government contractors use from time to time. It's called "contract modification." If the task is changing, if problems crop up on the job, if different specifications or parameters are insisted upon by the client, you come back with a request for a contract modification. "Yes, we did agree on this price, but we're going to have to modify this contract to complete the job." This way, you can renegotiate the price, lower the quantity, change the quality, or alter the deadline for delivery. Get the modification in writing during the project. Make the client sign an understanding that the changes have been agreed to. That way, you won't run into problems with the billing department after shipment. Keep your cool, try to work together, and you'll probably come to an agreement. If all else fails during a dispute, remember that something is better than nothing. Don't cut your own throat by fighting and ending up with not a red cent for the work you've done. Get your half of it, or your third, or your quarter, and cut 'em loose. You're an expert. You have more pressing business to attend to.

THERE IS A CERTAIN sub-species of problematic customer I label, "Mr. Kickback." Shoo him away instantly. When Mr. Kickback comes a-callin', he'll offer you visions of grandeur, of loads of easy money, of swift and slick ways of doing things. He came calling to me once. To save myself from a lawsuit, I can't mention the creature's name, but I can say his boss was Seal, the fine British singer. Seal happens to be a gentleman as well as an incredible artist, but the person who was working for him was cut from different fabric. This assistant had just joined the tour, and proposed to me that if he tossed all the printing and graphics business for Seal my way, I should give him ten percent of everything he spent on the account. What's more, he wouldn't argue any of the pricing. I could bill Seal for anything I wanted; the assistant would get his tithing. It was a "win-win" situation for the both of us.

It was the first time I'd been approached by this ilk. The decision was easy to make on moral grounds: reject the offer as if its maker were a leper. What confounded me was another factor: I wanted to get the tour. I briefly considered giving the assistant his ten percent while going about my business and not inflating my prices. In other words, I'd make 90 percent of my usual fees. Fortunately, the bad vibes from the offer ultimately made me reject it. I told him, flat out, that PERRi wasn't that type of business and he'd have to go to someone else.

There's nothing good about being dishonest anywhere, at any time, with whatever powers of rationalization are at your disposal. It's digging your own grave, just like lying. As it turned out, the unscrupulous aide got fired from the tour after a couple months. I never learned the reason, but strongly suspect he was playing his kickback game with others and simply got caught. PERRi ended up getting the Seal tour anyway. Which makes for a nice ending the anecdote. But something more needs to be said: you must learn the norms of the industry you're entering. While kickbacks are no-nos in the entertainment industry, there are such things in some industries as corporation rebates. If, for example, a restaurant buys a certain quantity of a catsup brand, it may receive a rebate. The difference is, the benefit accrues to the company, and it's legal, just like factory rebates when you buy a car. The bottom line: find out what is accepted custom among your customers. Then adhere to it.

NOW IT'S TIME TO deal with the second sector of money management: paying up. I happen to love mathematics. It was my favorite school subject. However, despite this propensity for playing with numbers, I prefer to spend my time looking for new customers and being more productive, rather than tending to bean-counting. So I hire a bookkeeping service.

Bookkeeping chores fall into three time frames: daily, monthly, and yearly. I take care of the daily paperwork — invoicing, purchase orders, and so on, but I hire a professional bookkeeper to handle my monthly paperwork: the payrolls, tax reports, workman's compensation, social security, and so on. For the yearly paperwork, particularly income taxes, I retain a certified public accountant to make sure the figures all add up and no aggressive audit will blow me out of the water. I work directly with the bookkeeper. The bookkeeper works directly with the CPA. It all works out perfectly.

For a very short period, I did my own bookkeeping. It proved tedious, not to mention troublesome if I fell behind on daily entries. Bookkeeping services, on the other hand, charge as little as $200 a month for a ten-employee staff, and ensure the details are done right, down to cutting payroll checks, calling on accounts receivable, and paying quarterly business tax.

When you hire a bookkeeper, be certain he or she is well-versed in taxes. Ask how many audits the bookkeeper has been through. The bookkeeper should have the name of the officer or officers who've done the audit or audits. I can't recommend a bookkeeping service enough for entrepreneurs handling a large client load. On the other hand, experts handling single contracts at a time can bypass the bookkeeper and work directly with the CPA. Retaining a CPA is critical. You'll need professional advice to find all the tax breaks and allowable expenses, as well as to avoid a costly audit down the road. Your bookkeeper and CPA — and your lawyer, if you have one — are as invaluable to your operation as your daily employees. This means that they stand at the top of the ladder when you're determining who gets paid first. You must also give top payment priority to the people you're using as trade references.

People considering doing business with you will likely ask for trade references. You'll furnish names of several vendors, suppliers, and service providers you do business with. Make sure you haven't missed any payments with these references. It's an easy error to commit; avoid it. It's only good business sense.

I mentioned earlier in the chapter that I prefer to bill long-term customers on a "net ten day" basis. As a billee, I like to set up payments on a 30- or 60-day schedule.

However, I only ask this of people whom I work with on an on-going basis, who show up with a delivery truck every week. Sometimes, long-term payment schedules can mean that days, weeks, or months slip away, and before you know it you're behind in your debt. So remember: if you are using a constant supplier as a trade reference, make sure you're never late with a payment. If you do a fair amount of business, you'll likely be issued a number by the Dun & Bradstreet credit-reporting service. Dun & Bradstreet contacted PERRi Entertainment before we were 6 months old. It did not charge us to maintain information about us in their service. We were happy to be included.

I went, one time, to lease a truck for my company. PERRi has very good credit with everyone we list as a reference. We have very good bank credit, as well. Nevertheless, the car company informed me that someone had reported my company to Dun & Bradstreet. I was surprised. I went back and learned that an employee had used our company name to purchase an airline ticket, and hadn't paid for the ticket. The travel agency reported us. A good thing to do is to call Dun & Bradstreet and obtain a quarterly report on who is talking about you to the service. It costs less than $100 a year, and it keeps you up to speed on how you look to others in the business world.

ALLOW ME TO PASS along a few final money management tips: A once-a-year review of your expenses, fees, and services is in order. I had fixed a certain price on my bead chains. We had tracked the price for a couple years to ensure we were earning sufficient markup. One day, a box of chains arrived. It felt as heavy as a brick. We determined how much we were being charged by the supplier to ship us the chains. The charges for two years turned out to be more than what we were buying the product for! Needless to say, we adjusted our prices on bead chains.

In sum, it is wise to take a step back once a year,

amid the engrossing pursuit of money, to assess what costs you're incurring, to calculate how much time you're spending on projects, and to analyze what you're charging people. It achieves nothing to bellyache about the IRS. It appears the American pastime these days is to gripe about paying taxes. The Internal Revenue Service seems to be universally vilified. Allow mine to be a rare voice of dissent in the wilderness: Pay the IRS, shut up, and spend your time doing hard work instead. If half the country did this, we probably wouldn't have such high taxes. I have yet to find any use in arguing with or fighting the IRS. You'll get nowhere. The energy expended battling Uncle Sam over tax audits could be fruitfully directed toward getting a new client whose business could pay the part of the tax bill you're contesting.

In line with this, I told my bookkeeper when we hired her to be sure we pay everything, and to not try to hide anything. If she thinks we may have to pay a use tax, then pay the use tax. Don't question anything. PERRi was audited for the first time in three years. Our fine: $13. We did very well. The auditor was pleased with us. He ended up writing a favorable report. We didn't set ourselves up to be picked on in the future.

Pay all your taxes, whether city, county, state, or federal, and you'll stay out of trouble. You'll also be able to focus your energy on getting good, healthy clients and building your business. In other words, on being productive.

Contracts or simplified written understandings are a good idea to secure before embarking on long-term projects. Let's say a county in California calls Glenn the contractor to serve as a consultant to provide an estimate on the costs to build a new correctional facility. Glenn figures it will take him two weeks to do the job. He'll ask, first, for a written understanding that spells out that his expenses and fees will be paid. Should the construction project go forward and

Glenn be hired to supervise the jail's construction, he will definitely require that a contract be signed.

Lawyers specializing in contracts are the ones to secure to hash through the documents and deal with the obligatory jargon. Written contracts are unnecessary, and likely impractical, for every single job you'll do, particularly for short-term or one-time jobs. And they are not always essential. A "contract" is established the moment someone has paid something. If Glenn the contractor has been billing a company for his hourly wages as senior project manager on the new county jail under construction, and the company has been paying on his invoices for, say, two months, then that's a kind of contract in itself. The county has recognized the fees it is paying Glenn; the amount is not going to change.

Finally, when it comes to contracts, I am a firm believer that you will have a good feeling about a customer that he or she is not going to burn you. This is not to say that you should never use contracts, because if you do harbor doubts about a client, it's not a bad practice to ask around about the person. Has he or she ever burned anyone? That will help you decide the right thing to do.

If you do end up getting burned, know that seeking legal remedy is often extremely difficult for the expert from out of town. Again, geography complicates the matter. Civil complaints must be filed locally. That means you'll have to travel to the city where your customer does business to file suit. And because you're from out of town, you will likely have to file a claim in another state, using a lawyer licensed in that state. It all becomes a major ordeal. It's too hard for you to pursue unless the sum due you is large enough to justify time spent trying to retrieve it. Think of it on a purely monetary basis. How much time is it going to take to sue this person, anyway? Are the legal fees worth it? Or does your motivation basically come down to "the principle of the thing?" That should be a red flag right there, folks. Vengeance is a double-edged sword, wounding the wielder as surely as the target. Why cut your own throat? Instead, cut your losses and keep moving forward to get ahead.

When the Rock 'N' Roll Hall of Fame reneged on its payment to us, we decided to put the whole sorry episode behind us. By taking the high road, we continued to devote our resources to serving good clients and coaxing more such clients.

IN THE LAST ANALYSIS, what has worked well for me is the practice of avoiding traps that can lead to legal wrangles. This entails sticking with strict payment terms, asking for advances, getting paid C.O.D., maintaining the façade, and positioning myself among honest, upstanding customers and suppliers. In other words, maintaining the proper professional attitude and exercising good business etiquette. Do so, and you won't have to hemorrhage any blood pursuing deadbeats all across the country.

Collecting bills can turn into a major migraine. Collection agencies normally aren't interested in taking on accounts of small operators, particularly those who are trying to collect payments from customers around the nation. If you try to collect on outstanding accounts yourself, you may violate laws you didn't even know existed. You could interfere with someone's right of privacy, and lose any chance at legal redress. Did you know that if someone asks you to only contact them by mail, you aren't allowed to telephone them anymore? It's amazing what legal land mines await you in trying to recoup what's owed. So why punish yourself?

A similar situation exists on the buying side. I have occasionally been provided with poor products and have refused to pay. Some vendors have ended up suing me and wasting my time further. Once, I bought printing services that I was very unhappy with. I ended up paying more than

$7,500 in attorney fees fighting over $42,000. It was a perfect blunder, and one I shall never repeat. In most legal conflicts, the two sides end up meeting in the middle, but since each incurs legal bills, it all ends up a lose-lose deal.
What I now do is pay for a poor product, then set the supplier free.

My philosophy: don't headache yourself with dealing with people you don't want to deal with. It's like wrestling with a skunk. Instead, gravitate to the good people, trust your instincts to avoid the bad people, sever ties with those who don't measure up, cultivate ties with those who do, and keep on moving straight ahead.

CHAPTER TEN
Keep on Trucking — Sales and Other Operations

At this stage, you must concern yourself with the day-to-day workings of your business. Stamina is everything. The daily rigmarole can be divided into two categories: dealing directly with customers, and the general business operations. Since you can't have a business without customers, we'll discuss that category first.

I assume that by now you know how to get customers. You're using all the techniques we've discussed to begin to build your base, and have absorbed the skills to keep clients happy and coming back, spreading your good name throughout the nationwide marketplace. Your business is stoked up like the boiler room of a train and is steaming down the tracks. Now you must concern yourself with keeping it chugging along. Referrals are the key.

Because you're an expert with a very refined niche, you operate in a little world of your own making, its borders are defined by the population of those who require your expertise. This is the long way of saying that a selective set of customers will engage your work. Since most of them will likely know each other, or of each other, word of mouth is the most effective medium by which your business will become known. Thus, referrals will be responsible for a surprising portion of your business. They make up approximately four-fifths of mine. They are perhaps the most critical factor that will guarantee the endurance of your enterprise.

There are booms and busts, peaks and valleys, rush times and slow, times in the life of every business. It's ebb and flow. But you didn't become an expert from out of town as a get-rich-quick scheme. This is no fly-by-night, pie-in-the-sky ruse you're trying to perpetrate upon the public. Rather, it's a get-rich-gradually strategy. That's why it's vital you stay the course, ride the roller coaster, and continue to build your business steadily, surely.

Referrals will be your life-blood. Referrals are practically the be-all end-all of your advertising. One ad in a trade newsletter may land you one customer. That customer can spread the word that eventually yields you four more customers. They pass on your good name and it leads, over time, to eight more customers. And so on in the pyramid effect. In fact, referrals can originate from seemingly indirect sources. Networking at conventions and trade shows can lead to referrals months or years later. Action begets action.

Consider how good fortune smiled on Bill, our wood sculptor, on one particular occasion. His clientele — art patrons with a specific interest in wood sculpture — are a specialized group, indeed. A gallery in Montana that carried his work made a sale of a large carving he had done of an Indian. The buyer brought the sculpture home, where it became a fixture. It caught the eye of a guest, who happened to be a vice president of a hotel-casino.

The gambling industry executive commissioned Bill to do a sculpture for one of the chain's resorts in Colorado. As part of the deal, Bill's name and the names of galleries carrying his work are displayed near the sculpture. Thousands pass by this sculpture every day. The moral of the story: your finished jobs, paid for and done with, will continue to reap dividends for you as your best advertisements. They build your reputation. They generate referrals.

On the other hand, one bad apple can spoil the whole bunch. It can lead to "negative referrals," to customers being warned away from approaching you. Word-of-mouth from the disenchanted travels like wildfire, even faster than kind words of fulfilled clients. The besmirching of your reputation can sabotage all your earnest efforts to build a business. That is why you can't easily afford any dissatisfied customers. This is a cold reality of doing business, particularly within the narrow niche you've carved out as the expert from out of town.

Yes, you will make mistakes in handling accounts. We all do. But it's better to lose money and never do business with a person again, than to leave him or her upset with you when a job is done. You're better off paying the person a check and letting him or her go, than leaving the person incensed and thinking dark thoughts about you that can last for years.

"Will you give me another shot?" or, "Can I credit you for your next job, do it for free?" are approaches I've taken with the occasional disgruntled patron. Of course, as I mentioned before, some customers will never be content with the work you do. "Toxic" people will seek you out, too, along with the majority of well-adjusted, normal customers. The idea is to never get in too deep with these energy drains. You try to detect "poison" accounts before you agree to take them on, so you can (politely, of course) turn them away or direct them elsewhere. If, however, you do get involved, you must finish up with them as quickly as possible, even if it means acquiescing to their unreasonable demands. Then "let your competition have 'em."

There is a great distinction between not taking a job and taking one on and then deciding to get rid of the client at the appropriate juncture. If you've taken the job, you better damn well make the client happy. That's what you've agreed to do. You can't afford to sully your track record. This extends to all accounts. There were times I bit off more than I could chew with a job that taxed our resources. I retrenched, deciding we would carry on even though we'd lose money on it. For I knew full well the job was too large and important for us to goof up and damage our good name.

Recently, we took on a job to print the passes to a convention of the College Music Journal (CMJ). Our supplier that printed an angel insignia, used in the re-entry portion of the passes, failed to produce the product on time for us. I concealed this information from my client, for it looks terrible to give excuses for a job running behind schedule. It was our problem, not the client's. Our client didn't need us to try and pass the buck.

"It's our fault, I'm extremely sorry," I told CMJ. I went as far as directing the client to invoice us for any costs incurred from the inconvenience we had caused. "I will credit this entire bill, I don't care what it is, to next year's conference," I said. "Give me next year's business, give me a chance to prove myself, I will give you next year's passes for free." My contact knew we were a reputable company.

As it turned out, I made absolutely the right move in not trying to shift the blame for the foul-up. The repercussions of not bending over backwards to please my client could have been grim, indeed. David Bowie ended up showing up at the CMJ convention. And PERRi Entertainment was poised to begin the printing for his upcoming tour. Had I not helped out my CMJ contact, she could have informed Bowie's people that PERRi goofed them over, and that could have torpedoed our Bowie tour account.

TRACKING WHERE YOUR REFERRALS are coming from can key you in to the nature of your market, and should be incorporated into your business schedule as your enterprise grows. What we do is call our customers and inquire if we may ask them three questions:

• "How did you find out about us?"

• "What's your address for our Christmas mailing?" (they provide a personal address instead of a corporate address).

• "If we sent you a questionnaire about us, would

you have the time to fill it out?"

Tracking is important to feed your own marketing know-how; it also acts, subtly, as a follow-up advertising technique to keep customers thinking about you.

It's very difficult for small companies with large client loads to call every single customer to perform tracking. I learned this when I decided nearly three years into PERRi's existence to see how my customers had first heard about us. We chipped away daily at the client list, and after eight months had contacted 400 clients. Since our volume of new accounts didn't abate (thank God), we continuously fell behind in our tracking . . . and I don't believe we'll ever catch up.

From those we did reach, we learned that 82 percent came to us via referral. The other 18 percent? They contacted us after reading trade and newsletter advertising or receiving promotional mailers. They started our referrals. At some point you, too, will need to take a group of clients, whether it be five or 100, and determine from them how they found out about you. It will help you tailor your advertising.

A final word on developing referrals: don't ignore your secondary markets. Yes, you are a specialist, tightly focused on your area of expertise. But there are bound to be sectors of customers who diverge somewhat from your typical client profile. Most of PERRi's markets fall within the international touring industry, but we also service radio stations, concert venues, and sporting teams. We strive to avoid the tunnel-vision of concentrating solely on the touring industry, while neglecting these other legitimate sectors. Remember: there are climbs and dips in business volume. Don't pooh-pooh the pursuit of less "sexy" accounts. They, too, are fuel to keep your business engine running all the time, instead of sputtering to a halt.

THE GRIND, THE DAY-TO-DAY operations of

business, should concern you as much as the hunt for customers. You must have a well-running engine to keep forging ahead. A top priority is having enough employees to handle your workload.

I may be an extreme example of a person who's always looking to hire more help. For example, not long ago I hired a new personal assistant. My bookkeeper and accountant both said I was crazy. "There aren't enough desks," they said; "there isn't even enough work for her at the moment." "Just calm down, Tony," they said. I have been accused of being go-go-go. I proudly cop to the charge. I am definitely a person who is moving ahead fast. If you want to catch the train, you better hop aboard now because we're heading nowhere but forward. My philosophy is that there is no reason to stand still. There is every reason not to.

At the other end of the spectrum is the person who lacks the nerve to expand his employee pool, and thus never grows his business. I have someone in mind who exemplifies this static state. I won't give his name, but I will say that he is a very nice and personable gentleman, with his own little advertising agency. The other day, he complained to me, "I just want to grow, but there's no time to even handle all the business I have now."

His payroll has listed but two employees for many years. He's never bitten the bullet and hired that third or fourth or fifth underling. He could even wade into growth by hiring an apprentice at a minimal salary, to gain a bit of breathing room to tackle more projects. If the apprentice worked out, then the agency owner could give him or her a raise and promotion, then take on enough additional accounts to justify another entry-level hire, and so on.

Expansion isn't for everyone. If you like staying small, great, but for those who yearn to grow, the old saying, "nothing ventured, nothing gained" holds true. I've learned that the more capable employees you have, the more money you'll automatically bring in, no matter your previous business volume. You may, in fact, be greatly surprised how your ability to make money by having more people — that is, to capitalize on the work of your employees — increases exponentially with each additional good hire. I like to put it this way: "people will cover their own." Good employees will pay for themselves, and then some. In sum: don't wait to make a mountain of money before you go out and hire more people. Hire more people to go out and make a mountain of money.

Sometimes I do worry that I'll be "ripped off" by my employees, training them only to watch them leave to start their own businesses. What I've done is have my employees sign short-term "non-compete" pacts that preclude them for a period of time from leaving me to start a rival enterprise or join a competitor.

When an employee does leave me, one of two things has happened: either he or she was fired for incompetence or unreliability; or the person did the work superbly and left to start a business after the period of non-competition expired. Those that were terminated can legally go to work for a competitor. Our Western legal tradition holds that a person cannot deny another his or her right to earn a living at his or her trade. However, I don't worry about what company secrets a terminated worker will take with him or her. If the person performed so poorly that I ended up divesting myself of his or her services, then I'm happy to "let the competition have 'em."

SEASONAL LULLS IN BUSINESS are bound to occur. Even our nation's economy has yearly swings, cranking up every November during the Christmas rush, then slowing down in January. Different industries experience different cycles. Bill the wood-carver's seasonal lull takes place every March through May. Every year, he has a real dead period as spring comes on. For some reason, it's just not a good time for people buying wood sculptures.

PERRi Entertainment's slow time runs from November through January, when concert tours have ended with the onset of fall, not to gear up again until spring. I remember gathering the troops into my office one December day, intending to give them a pep talk. "If there's any time of the year we don't want to be leaving early or coming in late because business is slack, this is it," I said. "This is the time of year to be marketing and going gung-ho and trying to find new customers, and coming in early and staying late!" My talk didn't work. My staff continued to skulk in late and sneak out early. So be it. There is such a thing as hibernation, and in letting up on your employees so they can enjoy the holiday season. Nevertheless, there are a couple things you, the boss, can do during the lulls.

It's a perfect time for you to re-engineer, to examine your business, think about your processes, bookkeeping procedures, management, and so on. Another thing you can do is examine your hard costs, see how you're billing, how much money you're making, how you are covering overhead, whether certain products are working out. It's not make-work. You're not keeping busy for the sake of keeping busy. It's important to periodically assess and analyze your operation. The seasonal hiatus provides the perfect opportunity to do this. On the other hand, if the lull is not seasonal in nature, but due to a lack of business or a slowing of the economy, then you must kick yourself in the seat and get out and market more.

Sometimes you will feel very isolated as the expert from out of town. You're so far removed from your clients. A lull can make you feel very much alone. If it's a seasonal lull, don't worry about it. If it's not a seasonal lull, worry about it. Get out and market!

Let me say this about the economy: downturns and recessions do happen, but take them with a grain of salt.

Yes, there are trends in housing sales and construction projects and retail business; yes, there are fluctuations in the values of currencies and commodities and oil. Often, however, you make your own economy. Hustle, and the work will be there for you.

A hedge against lulls is to save a little for the rainy days. An early partner of mine gave PERRi one of the best pieces of business advice we've ever gotten. I remember telling him once, "Every winter we have such a tough time with our books; we're so low on funds." His suggestion: every time we cut payroll checks during our flush periods, we should also cut a check to a savings account. We did this, and ended up with an additional $15,000 in the bank this year. It was a nice cushion. So prepare for slow seasons; don't wait for them to catch you short of cash. Some banks will make loans for seasonal lulls, provided they truly are seasonal lulls. You often won't be able to recognize what is a seasonal lull and what is a dry spell brought on by lack of aggressive and consistent marketing until you've been in business for three or four years and can identify such cycles. Keep graphs of your business activity. Lulls will be very pronounced on them.

If you are an expert who takes on a small number of long-term projects rather than a large number of short-term projects, then you'd be crazy to not continue to market while you're laboring through accounts. Failure to do so is an instant way to create a lull. Experts fall into this rut all the time. They become so wrapped up in the long-term projects that they neglect to devote a few hours each week to advertising themselves. A perfect example of this is the person who hires onto a big rock 'n' roll tour, with a Rod Stewart or a Billy Joel, and soon is making so much money out on the road that the person forgets to market himself or herself for the next tour. Inevitably, the long tour ends, and wham! — the person can be out of work for almost a year.

On the other hand, there are those who always

manage to hitch a new ride. I am sure they've been on the phone while still employed, connecting up toward the day the tour ends. Call them savvy. You must be, too.

THE NICE PART ABOUT having your business age, in watching the years pile up, is that you develop long-term relationships with customers and suppliers.

I mentioned in an earlier chapter that it's a good practice to maintain some degree of distance, of formality, between you and your business associates. It engenders mystique, and thus commands respect. However, there is much to be said about building up a history of working together, so a sense of closeness accrues.

The other day, I telephoned the Eagles' tour coordinator, Chris Littleton. There was no specific occasion; I had just been sitting at my desk when the thought flashed into my mind that he had been such a nice guy, so personable and easy to work with, when we'd done business together. So I called him just to thank him for his business. I had no ulterior motive. I wasn't checking to see whether the Eagles were going out again and if we could again have their printing account. It was just a friendly call.

Nurture long-term relationships. The value is priceless. It brings loyalty. It brings referrals. It gives you a good name in your industry. What's beautiful about building a long-term relationship is there's nothing phony or artificial about it. I can hardly think of one person with whom I've worked for years on end whom I haven't argued with at some point or other.

There is a gentleman named Alan Zullo. We first did business together when he managed a tour for Andrew Dice Clay. I believe the comedian's abrasive personality had rubbed off on Alan. When we were together, it was like each of us pulling the other's teeth. Neither of us cared to acquiesce to the other's stiff demands. It was like a spat between brothers. Brothers is a good word for it. For no matter how much we tussled, a real trust existed. And woe was he who tried to come between us. Alan and I — we could fight with each other, but you better not say one bad word about Alan Zullo to me. He was my buddy. We had bonded. When it comes to doing business, we're partners in crime. We still argue like mad. We recently bickered over a tour by the band Bush. "Alan, you got me down to doing the thing for barely nothing!" I said, but if an employee were to come to me and say, "Alan is giving us a hard time," I'd say, "Well, take care of him."

Yet, there is still that mystique, that cloak of mystery hanging between us. Alan Zullo and I do not talk about our families. We have not spent weekends together in Hawaii. Alan has never been to my home. In fact, we've met only a few times. The first time I was in New York City at a Bette Midler show at Radio City Music Hall. Alan was handling Bette's tour; I was backstage before she went on. I had come from several blocks away, where I was handling the work for a Paul Simon and Art Garfunkel show at Madison Square Garden's Paramount Theater. It was very short: "Hey, Alan Zullo! Tony Perry." We shook hands but nothing rubbed off. No mystique was shred.

Maybe that's why we continue to get along so well. We have long-term business loyalty, but we haven't personalized the relationship into a true friendship, and so we still recognize there is a line that can't be crossed. Neither is entitled to ask for special favors or use friendship as leverage to beat up the other on a deal. Call it respect. As long as I don't burn Alan Zullo, as long as I don't steal from his purse, I'll always get his business, and he's priceless not only as a customer, but as a reference. Long-term clients like him will keep referrals coming my way. They will level off the lulls in my business. Think of them almost as safety nets.

SUPPLIERS ARE ALSO TO be nurtured as loyal

business associates. PERRi Entertainment occasionally contracts out to a smaller printer certain large specialty jobs, such as numbering tickets.   Someone once asked me, "Tony, why do you only use one printer?" It's common for advertising agencies to use five, ten, 20 different printers. They'll hire out jobs on the three-bid system. The lowest bidder gets the job.

The reason I stick with one specialty printer is because I have developed a relationship that I have retired upon in a pinch. By throwing all my extra business to one printer, I knew I could count on that printer to get my work done right away on a rush job. There is no notion of being mercenary, of only using this printer because it was the lowest bidder on a particular job. I've earned the printer's trust.   There is mutual loyalty. When, in a crisis, we absolutely, positively have to have a job done this week, this printer has pulled through for us. (Don't be foolish, however, and not have a backup.)

There is a major concert promotion company that I'll call "Acme Promotions." Up until the death of its head person, the company seemed to be family oriented, committed to long-term associations. PERRi had done a lot of work for this company, but after a new leader came in, the personality changed and the company became colder, more detached to those with whom it had done business for so long. Then came the day we were told to bid on a ticket-printing job against two other companies. We were only to be used if we put in the doggone lowest price. This made us feel terrible, like our history with Acme meant nothing.

Acme knew we were competitive. Acme knew we were professional. Yet the company still wanted to go with the person with the lowest bid. It turned out our price was $6,000 above the lowest bidder. An Acme representative called in anger. "How could you be this much more expensive? Have you been inflating your prices all along?" I said I'd review the costs. I found they added up.

"This is the price, we're holding to it," I said. Acme went elsewhere for the account. I figured we had been way undercut by another printer that wasn't making any money on the job, but just wanted Acme's business. That had to be the only explanation. No one could work that cheaply.

We felt very badly. We couldn't believe Acme had no loyalty to us. Didn't the company realize that if the cost was $6,000 below ours, something had to be wrong? Well, something was wrong. The lowest bidding printer had erred in its calculations. It had totaled up a price based upon 100 sheets of stock, believing it was the price for 1,000 sheets. When it went to buy its supplies for the printing job, it was $12,000 *over* our price.

Acme called us back. Now the account was ours, but believe me, there was a bitter taste in our mouths. We were quite disenchanted by this point. The relationship had been compromised. We felt cheated upon. What's more, Acme's people had wasted four weeks with the other printer, and now wanted us to pull rabbits out of a hat for them. They needed the generic tickets produced in five days.

We did the work, but gave it no special consideration over other customers. Lucky for Acme, we weren't already engaged in other rush jobs. Acme wouldn't have been given top priority. The point to all this is: take care of your suppliers. They're your business's life-line.

REMEMBER: EVERY TIME YOU sell a job to a customer, you're not just selling your business's work, you're selling your relationships with your suppliers. If they can't come through for you, you can't come through for your customers. No business is an island onto itself. Flout your associations with your suppliers, and you're diminishing yourself.

Every business has suppliers. Even if you're just typing résumés, you have to buy paper from someone. Take care of your suppliers. They're people hustling to make a living just as you are. And when you're scrupulous, they're scrupulous. What's more, there will come a day when you'll need a favor from them. If you've been nickel-and-diming them forever, they won't come through for you.

Let's say Glenn the jail-builder uses a special electric eye for his projects. There is an ugly riot one day in a jail Glenn built, and numerous electric eyes are destroyed. If every time he built a jail, Glenn had beat up his electric eye manufacturers, made them bid low to win accounts, they won't look too affectionately upon him when he calls to say he has to replace one of his project's electric eyes in a hurry. "Oh, here's Glenn the chiseler," they'd think. "The warranty's up, Bud. Go call the other guys you had bid the job. Ask them to fix it." But if Glenn had faithfully patronized one electric eye company the entire time, you can bet he'll be taken care of. Glenn will have become a regular. He will have his own "stool at the bar."

Let me end this chapter with a true anecdote.

PERRi Entertainment uses only one foil supplier, Crown Roll Leaf. The special foiling material or holograms on tickets and security credentials on the printing we produce all comes from Crown Royal Leaf. One day we were toiling away on a parking credentials job for a new client, the Super Bowl champion San Francisco 49ers, when we suddenly ran out of foil. With the deadline approaching, we were in a crunch! Crown Royal recognized that in the past we had tossed it business on big accounts, such as the Rolling Stones. I called and got the owner on the line. He ended up staying late, and got the product out to us. Would he have done this had I not given him dedication and support throughout the years? Probably not. Instead, he personally kicked butt for us. He went to the wall for us because we had been using him exclusively.

We finished our job for the San Francisco 49ers on time. This most prestigious client of ours was quite pleased, which, we believe, will mean more business for us down the line. And more referrals, so that we can keep on trucking along. It all fits together, doesn't it?

CHAPTER ELEVEN
Some Actual Experts From Out of Town

Throughout the book, I have alluded to three hypothetical experts from out of town to illustrate various points. Now it is time to let you in on a little surprise: they are actual people. There really is a "Glenn the jail builder." His name is Glenn Burner, and he is a contractor who hires himself out as a senior project manager to large construction companies who have contracts to build prisons.

Likewise, there is a "travel agent to the stars" named Lorrie. She is Lorrie Haimes, whose Entertainment Travel By Lorrie, Inc., is based in Seminole, Florida. There is also a wood sculptor, specializing in Indian carvings, up in little Lakeview, Oregon. He is Billy Gerber, and he bills his "Gerber Originals" as, "one of a kind wood and antler carvings." Following are sketches of each.

GLENN BURNER RETURNED FROM Army service in Vietnam in 1969 and two years later, his four-year military stint completed, went back to his home town of Phoenix.

Growing up, Burner had wanted to be a machinist or mechanic. Out of the service, he cast about for a trade. He joined the Cement Finishers Union and went to work for McCarthy Western Construction, a major general contractor that had bought out a local contractor.

It turned out that Burner stayed with McCarthy for 17 years, rising through the ranks and mastering his profession. Early on, he completed an apprenticeship program and joined the Carpenters Union. By 1979, he had attained the level of superintendent. Burner proved a terrific asset for McCarthy. He had been brought up to work hard, be honest and sincere. He was always driven to do a good job. One key trait that stood him in good stead was that he could motivate people, inspiring them to perform tasks they hadn't believed they could accomplish.

He could be sent into a territory where McCarthy had

won a project bid but wasn't yet known to the local construction community, and pull together the disparate players into a tight, cohesive team. He always assembled a crew that got the job done. Because of this, a McCarthy executive nicknamed him, "Glenn the Gunslinger." The moniker has stuck.

McCarthy is a general contractor specializing in heavy concrete buildings —what is known as heavy construction. Correctional facilities involve a lot of concrete. Therefore it followed that McCarthy bid on jail projects. Burner soon found himself in a supervisorial role building a jail. He was the concrete superintendent building Florence State Prison, about an hour's drive east of Phoenix. In time, Burner was appointed the project superintendent on a maximum security federal facility being built north of Phoenix. When McCarthy began bidding on jail projects outside Arizona, Burner found himself relocating every couple years to a new site.

His first out-of-state jail project was supervising the construction of the Lerdo Pre-trial Jail Facility in Bakersfield, California. It took about 26 months. Then Burner was sent to Pasadena to supervise a retirement center project. After that, there was a parking structure in downtown Los Angeles, but constructing correctional facilities became Burner's passion. Each jail or prison is geared to specialized purposes and demands; jails and prisons don't fall into a broad category that beckons repetitive designs to be replicated from project to project across the country. Burner likes that they are usually built in isolated areas away from population centers. He also likes the challenge each one presents, for correctional facilities require every facet of construction. They are to house people year-round, 24 hours a day, and are rather self-contained with their own hospital facilities, educational areas, housing, and security arrangements. They are very sophisticated constructions.

He also likes the pressure of coming onto a job where his reputation precedes him — where all an employer knows about him is that he's been successful on other jobs (Mystique! — Chapter Two) — and taking charge of a project where millions of dollars are involved and he is the point man to bring the project to fruition. "Pressure is good, it motivates me," Burner says.

His is a very demanding industry. For example, the state of California is under federal court order to have correctional facilities built to alleviate overcrowding in its prison system. Across the country, there is a large construction market in building prisons. Construction companies soon took note of Burner's expertise. That is how he has positioned himself in the construction industry as the expert in supervising the building of penal institutions (Finding your niche! — Chapter Three). He was able to leave McCarthy Western Construction in 1988 and become the expert from out of town.

Today, there are perhaps a dozen people in Burner's category who are experts in supervising the construction of prisons and jails. Burner has never had to aggressively market himself within his niche. His field, especially in the West, is a tight circle, and his good name is well known. His jobs have come to him via word of mouth. Typically, Burner will get a call from a previous employer, asking what he's working on, telling him about a project that is proving difficult and asking whether Burner's interested in it.

What's more, Burner never suffers a lull in his business. He always has a new job lined up before the present one is finished (Marketing! — Chapter Six). Because jail construction is so diversified an undertaking, incorporating every aspect of construction, the person experienced in supervising such projects is qualified to take on just about any other kind of construction project.

Jail-building is not just highways or bridges or warehousing. In between jail projects, Burner has helped supervise building a hospital in northern Nevada. But jail-building is his thing. When it comes to correctional facilities, Burner has eight such projects under his belt, from Arizona to California to Massachusetts to Missouri to Florida. He is a "can-do" guy who says he doesn't take "I can't" from anyone. That is how he proves an effective administrator on jobs that average about 150 employees. Such a skill keeps him in demand.

3D International hired Burner to supervise the building of Ione State Prison outside of Sacramento. Then Sumitomo Construction America Inc. engaged his services to manage the building of the ten-story San Mateo County

Jail addition in Redwood City, California. As of this writing, Burner is supervising a 22-month project for Kajima Construction and Engineering Inc., building the medium-maximum security facility, Soledad II, in Monterey County, California.

Actually, Burner wasn't the original supervisor. The project was underway and not going well, so Kajima hired Burner to come in and set things right. Characteristically, Burner didn't seek out this job. In fact, he had never even heard of Kajima. Contractors working on the site knew him and recommended him to the construction company. In turn, Burner maintains excellent relations with contractors and sub-contractors, such as electrical or plumbing companies (Keeping your suppliers happy! — Chapter Nine).

Burner is active in the industry. He attends American Concrete Institute meetings, and keeps abreast of new technology at trade shows. He is well-connected in construction, particularly in Arizona, Nevada, California, Oregon, and Texas. He helps out contractors, instead of running them out of business by monopolizing projects and employing only a few. "We're constantly scratching each other's backs, that's how you get this stuff done," Burner says, "even though the paperwork trail (the documentation) is monstrous."

Burner has a loyal cadre of managers — a superintendent, engineer, and assistant project manager — whom he works well with and likes to bring to new projects. He calls them "my old buds."

One thing Burner doesn't do is let himself be taken advantage of. His reputation as a straight shooter is everything to him. One time, a city building inspector said, "Glenn, you wouldn't have any trouble getting your building passed inspection through the city inspection department. My boss needs a new Cadillac." Burner threw him out of his office: "Get out of here, don't come back." Rejecting "Mr. Kickback" ended up causing Burner some frustration, because his inspections became, in his words, "double-tough." But Burner had his honor and integrity intact. He says he still must face sleazy offers from time to time, but he's a "real honest person," he says. His mother even tells him he's honest to a fault. "My word is still my word,"

Burner says, "and the people who know me in this business respect it, and know if I give my word, I'll do it." Burner's integrity, expertise, and renown within his industry guarantee he'll be a busy expert jail-builder for years to come.

"ONE DOESN'T WAKE UP one day and say, 'God, I just want to be a travel agent!'," Lorrie Haimes says. "It's not something that pops into one's head." But here she is: owner of the successful Entertainment Travel By Lorrie, Inc., in Seminole, Florida, handling the ticketing and lodging needs for entertainers from across the country — and world. In fact, Haimes' young enterprise grossed more than $1 million its very first year in operation. "The impossible we can handle," reads a trade magazine advertisement for her business. "Miracles take a little longer."

Truth be known, says the 35-year-old Haimes, she got into the travel business quite by accident. But it so happens that one part of the equation, a background and interest in entertainment, was already in place. Haimes' family, along with singer Joey Dee (Joey Dee & the Starliters had a string of early-1960s hits, including the "Peppermint Twist" and "Shout"), started the National Music Foundation. The Foundation funds a rest home for aging rock 'n' rollers. Haimes was, at the time of its planning, running her stepfather's dental office.

One day, her stepfather, Alan Haimes, and Joey Dee were with a couple of other people in the office, discussing how they were interested in building a retirement facility for the pioneers of rock 'n' roll. Each was highly enthusiastic about the notion and discussed writing the initial letters. This is where Lorrie got involved: "Guys, give it to me, I'll help you." The next thing she knew, she was neck-deep in the project.

Haimes met the "Dick Clarks" of the industry — the bedrock veterans who had become large successes — and the legions of early rockers who had been told in their heyday to sign on the dotted line and they would become rich. Only they hadn't become rich — or even financially comfortable. Now they were in their 60s. Many had been "one-hit wonders" in their youth; others had maybe had a bit more musical success, yet neither group saw much in the way of financial rewards for all their efforts. They didn't have much more to go on than fond memories and, perhaps, a lingering ability to perform.

Haimes came to meet many of the grizzled rockers. Within two years, announcer/entrepreneur Dick Clark of "American Bandstand" fame became chairman of the board of the National Music Foundation. The enterprise was kicking into high gear, and fund-raising concerts became the need of the moment.

A well-known New York promoter took Haimes under his wing as his only protégé. In this way, she listened in on contract negotiations, gained road experience on tours, and even began to negotiate acts and the use of concert venues. Haimes loved working behind the scenes, organizing events, putting all the pieces together. To this day she relishes being what she terms a "professional troubleshooter." "Give me the problem and I'll fix it," she says. "I thrive on that."

At 31, Haimes, for personal reasons, decided it was time to move on from the National Music Foundation. Like many facing an occupational change, she found herself at a crossroads. There she was, a divorced, single mother with a 3-year-old and an infant, and no clear direction where to head for a career. One yearning she had was to become a prosecuting attorney, but Haimes had no time to go back to school. Fortunately, it seems Gary Puckett (of Gary Puckett & the Union Gap) had become good friends with Haimes, and he had a wonderful suggestion: why shouldn't she go into management, coordinating acts on tour? Puckett recalled how efficient Haimes had proved in handling travel logistics for National Music Foundation benefits, facilitating band members' schedules so they would land and depart on time to meet concert dates. It was clear to Puckett that Lorrie had the knack. (Knowledge! — Chapter Three.) So she tried being travel coordinator for various acts. She hated it. Earning five percent commissions on airline tickets was not a sufficient living for her.

It so happened that she had a friend who owned a travel agency. Haimes tried that route: signing on as an agent. That didn't suit her, either. She had no self-confidence. She believed she had no aptitude for the job.

She quit and was out of work for six months.

In 1991 after Haimes had sold off her art work and jewelry, she realized that she needed a job, so she returned to her friend's travel agency. This time — to her great and pleasant surprise — her experience was entirely different. All of a sudden, she discovered she was good at the work (Mastering! — Chapter Three.) Haimes found herself proficient at getting her customers, in her words, "from A to B in a cheap, orderly fashion."

With $2,000 borrowed from a friend to buy equipment and open her own office, Haimes took a chance in July 1994 and formed Entertainment Travel By Lorrie, Inc. She soon capitalized on the connections she made through the National Music Foundation, but she had to beg for her first official account. It turned out to be Rob Grill, lead vocalist with the Grass Roots.

"Well kid, why should I use you?" he demanded.

"Because I need a break!" she answered.

"Well, I have a travel agent," Grill said.

But Haimes persisted. She called the singer again three weeks later. It so happened that Grill's agent had messed something up. Haimes was hitting him at the right time. Said Grill: "I'll give you one shot, kid. And I'm not going to talk to you but one time. You'll have to talk to my road manager from now on, because I don't do this."

Today, Grill is still Haimes' favorite account. And she talks only to him, not his road manager. What's more, Grill has referred many new accounts to her (Networking! — Chapter Six). Haimes comes through for all of them. There was the time, for example, when an entertainer called and said, "Oh, my God, we signed a contract. We thought it was this Saturday and it's really a Wednesday and now we're not making as much money as the air fares are." Haimes took the band's $7,000 travel budget and got the four guys to the same destination for only $802. It gave her an immense feeling of professional pride, even though a colleague criticized her for losing out on a lot of commission money by downscaling the service. Haimes replied that, no, she was more interested in looking long-term. This strategy is easy to understand, for relationships and reputation are everything to a specialist with a narrowly defined niche.

Though Haimes is based in Florida, much of her

business is in Los Angeles. She is mobile. Her clientele reaches her, too, from distant points. Haimes recently received a fax from a promoter in Germany, buying plane tickets for an act in Maui. "I heard you can really do a great deal," he told her.

Haimes counts as one strength the fact she has never attended a travel agent school. Instead of relying only on punching up keys on a computer to find out what's available, she thinks laterally, like a detective, ferreting out options that aren't immediately apparent. Haimes is also cognizant that one must love what one does to succeed at it (Passion! — Chapter Three). That, too, is one of the keys to her success, she says.

Haimes gains great satisfaction from helping her clients out. She never looks at what's in a sale for her, but how the client can best be served. This philosophy is rooted in a special faith: that doing good always comes back to you. Her motto is, "Call me and tell me if you've got a problem."

It so happened that drummer Micky Dolenz's manager called Haimes one day with a problem. The ex-Monkees' itinerary and travel arrangements didn't mesh. No one, it seemed, had bothered looking at this man's schedule before booking his commitments. Dolenz's list of dates were faxed to Haimes, to see if she could set things straight. She quickly noticed that he was to be in Saskatoon, Canada, on one day, and on top of the World Trade Center in New York City the next. On the face of it, there seemed no way to feasibly accomplish this task, short of making time stand still! Haimes telephoned Dolenz's people and brought this situation to their attention. She could detect panic in their voices when they said they'd call her right back. When they did, they relayed the information that it would cost $14,000 to charter a plane to get Dolenz to his New York concert. What's more, the concert was a CBS Records affair, and Dolenz absolutely couldn't just not show up.

Haimes labored for three hours over the conundrum that night. Using all her travel agent wiles, she came up with an intricate plan involving jets and limousines, and even backups. Total price: $3,000. Haimes didn't earn a nickel from her work on that deal, but she got a charge out of doing a job well done. What's more, she rested assured that the next time the Monkees reunited, they'd be calling her to handle their travel arrangements.

When Haimes first opened shop, she did everything by herself and, she says, the crushing load nearly killed her. Slowly, she expanded with employees to three, adding two more in peak season. She used lots of business savvy in those early lean days. For example, she negotiated her long-distance telephone rates: something few people know is possible. "Most people don't know they're paying on average 25 to 32 cents a minute on their long-distance calls," Haimes says. "I got mine down to 13 cents a minute, incoming and outgoing, across the board." It counts a lot to her. In peak season, her phone bill reaches $1,500 a month. It would be double had she not talked her rate down.

Haimes' networking has progressed to a large degree by word of mouth. Clients have included Dion, the late Wolfman Jack, Barry White, the Spinners, the Turtles, Johnny Rivers, Peebo Bryson, a number of country and Christian bands, and various promoters, including one in Jakarta, Indonesia. There is no border to Haimes' territory; all she and her customers need to do business is a phone and a fax (Stay where you are! — Chapter Five).

Haimes hasn't met most of her customers, yet has developed "close working relationships" with most merely by working with them over the phone. Because of her experience in the entertainment world, she has proved capable of going to lengths other agents can't. "I'll find replacements for people if a band member is sick, because I know so many people," Haimes says. "It's those kinds of things I'll do that other agents can't or don't have the ability to do. You can't find a Hammond B3 organ? I'll find you one."

It fits completely into the characteristic profile of the expert from out of town that none of Haimes' business comes from her own town. Rob Grill, who lives in Orlando, Florida, is the closest account to her business. Doesn't surprise Haimes any. "How many entertainers do you know who are from Seminole, Florida?" she asks with a laugh.

BILLY GERBER OF LAKEVIEW, Oregon, calls himself a wood sculptor. He's been wood sculpting since 1973, and full-time since 1985. His business card, emblazoned with a gold stamp of a bald eagle descending with talons poised, reads: "Gerber Originals, one of a kind wood and antler carvings." But Gerber, 44, didn't start out working artistic wonders with wood, nor did he even set his sights on earning his living as an artist.

Gerber was a bartender for seven years, and a house-builder for another seven. The seeds for his artistic interest, however, had already been sown in college. There, he did foundry work; that is, he cast metals. After college, however, Gerber had no access to a foundry, so he started "playing around" with carving wood (Passion! — Chapter Three.) His interest in this medium hasn't wavered since. Gerber's passion for working with wood is powerful; even if, as a soft-spoken individual, he expresses his love in understated fashion: "It's really a challenging experience." He favors pieces with American Indian motifs, and wild animals.

Gerber's carpentry work, building houses, satisfied his creative drive for a time. He'd incorporate designs into his craft. "But I kept having this art come back and haunt me," he says of his consuming yen to carve wood sculptures. Gerber came to realize he was an artist more than a craftsman.

Slowly, it turned out that he was devoting more and more time to carving wood figures and selling them, and less and less time on carpentry jobs. He got to the point where he realized he could earn a livable income at wood sculpture, selling and shipping his products from Lakeview. (Stay where you are! — Chapter Five). Nevertheless, it took him about three years before he had built up the confidence to decide whether to continue as a carpenter or fully commit to being a sculptor. He had, after all, a wife and two children to support. He had to be sure of what he was doing.

In 1985, Gerber finally decided to pursue his art full-time. In retrospect, he comes to this conclusion: "If you have the determination to do something like this, the determination is every bit as important as talent; maybe even more so" (Don't psyche yourself out! — Chapter Four). Gerber began to travel to trade expositions, which ranged from craft shows to fine-art shows. These weren't catch-all affairs where anyone could exhibit. Most were selective; juries voted artists in. Some shows were very high-end.

Gerber remembers bronze pieces featured with asking prices of $100,000. Top-notch dealers came to these affairs. That was to Gerber's advantage (Trade shows! —Chapter Six).

He continued the road work for about three years. In time, Gerber landed some of his smaller pieces in two out-of-town galleries. He found that they sold better outside of Lakeview; and the money was better, too. "People's concept of money in Lakeview isn't the same as it is somewhere else," he politely explains. Nevertheless, the thought of basing himself somewhere other than Lakeview never entered his mind. "Every time I leave here, it's like I can't wait until I get back," he says. Gerber went back East one year, and was startled to find that so many people existed. He was glad to return to little Lakeview, which he calls, "the middle of nowhere."

There is an unexpected, added dividend to producing handmade art in an isolated locale such as Lakeview. Gerber, not being exposed to other artists, is forced to come up with his own inspiration and ideas. The result: his work bears an original stamp. Galleries agree. His art is one-of-a-kind. It certainly helps his sales. Lakeview is also important from another standpoint: the surrounding land provides the wealth of material for Gerber's work. Not only the juniper wood he favors, but abundant deer antler and rib bone.

Today, Gerber's unique work is carried by eight galleries around the nation. He continues to represent himself rather than go through an agent. By occupying such a refined niche in the art world, Gerber commands not only a market all his own, but considerable mystique. His "networking" has consisted solely of referrals. Most of the galleries who display his art have approached him, rather than the other way around. Gallery owners are ever on the lookout for new, fresh and interesting geniuses. They spot Gerber's work and can't wait to contact him.

Gerber refuses to go on consignment. His remote base precludes him from traveling frequently to keep tabs on how his work is selling — so he quotes a gallery a price on an item and sells it straight out. This may prevent him from earning a higher figure down the road when a piece sells; but it's how Gerber must work his one-man operation. His firm policy on selling directly to dealers can hardly be termed unfair, however. Gerber endeavors to set such prices on his work that the dealers can earn as much from a sale as Gerber does in parting with a piece. He readily acknowledges that some people disagree with this philosophy, and insist the artist should earn more than the dealer. But Gerber says, "If a dealer's willing to buy it from me, and if I'm happy with the price, then he may put two times as much of my work on the market." Works out for everyone.

Gerber spends no time on direct marketing. His advertising consists of a supply of business cards. He's intended to come up with a brochure; but he's simply been too busy. His sculptures are slowly produced and he admits to being "so far behind in orders" that he has scant time for other business-related activity. Gerber does intend to work into his schedule the production of larger pieces. He knows that when those bigger-ticket items reach the marketplace, they create a buzz — they advertise themselves — and their sales justify producing yet more of them.

Gerber has eased into a natural business cycle. Most of his orders come in May. By the time he gets them taken care of, it's October and another spate of orders is coming in to meet the Christmas rush. In between, Gerber fields individual orders, often cautioning customers he may not get to them for a year.

Perhaps his most fruitful single "marketing" experience was selling a larger-than-life wood sculpture of a bighorn sheep, its fleece intricately and painstakingly carved from deer horn, to Harvey's hotel-casino in Central City, Colorado. The bighorn sheep is the Colorado state animal. Gerber's sculpture, which the resort commissioned after representatives caught eye of his work in a California gallery, is displayed just inside the main casino entrance. The ram sculpture has generated even more business for Gerber, in a pattern he terms a chain reaction. A gallery in Aspen, not far from Central City, ordered more of his art.

A decade after finally taking the plunge as a full-time wood sculptor, Billy Gerber has grown used to shipping his art out to points from California to Colorado to Montana to Indiana and to Virginia. Much of his business is repeat; some customers are up to four or five Gerber originals.

Practice makes perfect, and beyond perfection, Gerber moves to conquer new techniques. He's always growing, which is important as an artist and as a businessman. Gerber is working up to producing seven or eight life-sized sculptures a year, something that would have been inconceivable when he started out as a professional. He can now look inside a chunk of wood and see a pattern much more quickly than he could a decade ago. "I'm getting to where I can visualize what I'm doing way better, because I'm doing it so much," he says. His expertise has grown.

Gerber, perhaps because he's an artist with a singular style and niche, is somewhat of an anomaly as an exemplar of the entrepreneurial specialist. He eschews trade magazines; he has no interest, or need even, to tap into the art world around him, save for maintaining relationships with the galleries that purchase his work.

THE LESSON HERE WITH Billy Gerber is that experts from out of town do run the spectrum. Not every one will expand his or her business by revving onto the information superhighway; or by carefully studying the nationwide market and preparing direct-mail advertising campaigns. But, the commonalities among successful experts from out of town are profound: a love of what they do, a mastery of what they do, a burning desire to succeed at what they do, and a year-in, year-out commitment to what they do.

Glenn Burner, jail builder.

Lorrie Haimes, travel agent for touring entertainers.

Billy Gerber, wood sculptor.

They have more in common than each probably realizes. Above all, they're fulfilled. And society is three experts richer for it.

CHAPTER TWELVE
Top 20 Fields Begging for Experts From Out of Town

It is amazing how many fields exist for would-be experts from out of town, once you've opened your eyes. Consider the <u>Yearbook of Experts, Authorities & Spokespersons: an Encyclopedia of Sources</u> (published by Broadcast Interview Source, 2233 Wisconsin Ave. N.W., Washington, D.C., 20007; telephone 202-333-4904; website http://www.yearbooknews.com). The 1996 version is a 2-inch, 1000+ page trade paperback guide to experts around the country.

This reference book, in fact, is a Who's Who of specialists, catalogued by occupation. One can find experts in such rarefied nooks of knowledge as Houdini's seance, homosexuals in the military, the Endangered Species Act, and taxation of the family. Category subtitles include bed and breakfasts, cable television, camping, cars, chefs, child care, criminal law, and on through the alphabet. The table of contents alone numbers 195 pages, from "A Course in Miracles" to "Zoos" (which lists eight world-renowned zoo experts).

I've leafed through the book for my own amusement and marked entries that caught my eye. They demonstrated the unlimited possibilities for finding areas of expertise. For example, Jack Olender, a Washington, D.C.-based lawyer, is a consultant on malpractice whose clientele consists of doctors who work in hospitals. Meanwhile, SWS Security is a Maryland-based manufacturer of electronic surveillance equipment, primarily for governmental agencies.

Then there is Richard Carleton Hacker, of Beverly Hills, California. He is "the Cigar Czar." As his advertisement in the book says, Hacker is, "The world's most entertaining author/spokesperson on cigar smoking." I love it! I can bet you any sum that Mr. Hacker would not survive long by peddling his knowledge solely in his own back yard — interest would wane rather quickly once the novelty wore off. So he's gone worldwide. After mastering (the "M" in the M.E.S.H. theory) he expanded his territory, then sharpened in and hyped himself. Hats off to Mr. Hacker.

Allow me to introduce Roger Snowden (1-800-32-ROGER), the expert at . . . bingo! Mr. Snowden is a distinguished-looking older gentleman with a beard. He has a newspaper, the Bingo Bugle, authors books, gives talks to cruise ship passengers, and offers himself as an interview subject to television and radio. He even produces and sponsors annual world-championship tournaments. Talk about taking your passion and capitalizing on it to make it your career.

I am also fond of the entry by Jim Tice, based in Beverly Hills (310-281-7478), whose company, Finders Keepers, is a global search service: "Searching for the stuff that dreams are made of." Tice is an expert seeker for customers with unusual requests. "Where do you go to locate an authentic Howdy Doody rocking chair?" his ad reads. "Where do you find a 350-pound woman to dance nude on a trampoline in a slow-motion scene for a scientific film on the study of motion?" (People magazine wrote of "supersleuth" Tice: "The search isn't over until the fat lady springs.")

Tice has located thousands of oddities, antiques and unique people for his customers. His ad portrait shows him sporting a fedora, above the tag line, "I'm glad I found ya!" He will gladly hire himself out as a speaker at your next social engagement.

The <u>Yearbook of Experts, Authorities & Spokespersons</u> is a veritable potpourri of professional pundits. Some have very broad areas of knowledge. Others, very narrow ones. Jeff Lotman is an internationally known collector of animation art — the hand-made drawings, or "cells," of vintage cartoons. That's a narrow field. But Nancy Baggett of Maryland (410-750-7048) is an expert on healthy cooking. This is a broad field. Ms. Baggett could, I'm sure, profit by staying regional instead of going national, given the wide market for her wisdom.

Similarly, Deborah Willoughby of Honesdale, Pennsylvania is a general expert on yoga. She is the editor of "Yoga International" — "the authentic source of yoga science and practice." Note that Ms. Willoughby did not limit her niche to specific yoga applications, such as yoga for geriatrics or for sports medicine. On the other hand, Donald Dossey, Ph.D., a psychologist based in Asheville, North Carolina, didn't go the route of taking on everything from marriage counseling to testing juvenile delinquents. His ad reads: "Whether curious about disaster stress, stress surrounding a holiday, or simply interested about humorous superstitious 'cures,' Dr. Dossey is a consummate reference for holiday superstitions and scientific tips to overcoming anxiety and stress." Dossey is founder of the Phobia Institute and Stress Management Center. He has all the "good luck" he needs.

In sum, the <u>Yearbook of Experts, Authorities & Spokespersons</u> lists experts on divorce and on dancing dolphins, air conditioning and interior design. The deep message here is that the possibilities for specialization are infinite.

YOU NEED NOT ORDER a copy of the <u>Yearbook of Experts, Authorities & Spokespersons</u> to get your brain cells crackling over the opportunities out there for the incipient expert from out of town. Just pick up a copy of your local telephone company's Yellow Pages. But the lesson there is how so many people — unlike those in the <u>Yearbook of Experts, Authorities & Spokespersons</u> — limit themselves to one town, while not defining their specialties to distinguish themselves from competitors. It is as if they haven't realized they live in the world's largest economy, the United States of America's, and that they can reach a vast market through such standard tools as the mail system, telecommunications, and the Internet.

The Nevada Bell Yellow Pages in my home town, Reno, list four pages of accountants. It amazes me to see how many bean-counters are fighting over the same mole-hill of beans. What if, say, just one of these accountants happened to be a boating lover? This person could conceivably orient himself or herself toward being a specialist in bookkeeping for marinas, yacht clubs, and the like.

Still in the "A's" of the Yellow Pages, I come to "Advertising." Again, four pages list agencies and consultants. All battling over the same accounts! What a perfect industry to specialize in! Advertising would seem to be a wide-open market. Imagine: the advertising specialist for automobile repair shops. Or for community churches. Dare I mention how many pages list attorneys? Sixty-five. Are there really that many ambulances to chase, marriages to bisect, criminals to cut deals for?

Still in the "A's" and . . . what's this? A gentleman with a helicopter service has taken out a four-color half-page ad, touting his load-lifting service. This is a very expensive ad. He's trying so hard to corner the Reno construction market for his service. What if he had focused his energy regionally? He could fly his chopper up and down the West Coast, hoisting tonnage for all sorts of customers. His ad dollar could go farther with a concentrated marketing campaign.

Let's take a peek at the "C's." There are 14 pages of carpet cleaners, and four pages of carpet sellers. I know from being in the entertainment industry that there is an outfit that specializes in designing and fabricating carpeting for entertainment arenas, large buildings, and special events across the country. At a recent convention, I marveled at how many patrons visited this company's booth. Clearly, no one was going to pull the rug out from under them in their tightly focused field.

Electricity . . . Paving . . . Roofing . . . Tiling . . . Uniforms.

I know of a company that advertises frequently in Nightclub & Bar magazine, that only makes uniforms for cocktail waitresses. It has the right idea. What has separated it from the legions of seamstresses, tailors, and textile merchants? The willingness to specialize, and to expand nationwide.

Video stores? The Nevada Bell Yellow Pages list six pages of these in Reno. If you happen to own one and are tired with fighting for the leisure dollar in your community, renting out Stallone, Arnold, or Whoopi Goldberg flicks, think about specializing in one aspect of this business. I know of a business, Digital Business Systems, in Las Vegas that has positioned itself as the expert in setting up computer systems for video stores. That is what is known as sharpening in on an area of expertise.

All these accountants, ad agencies, attorneys, and on through the alphabet in the Yellow Pages are fighting for business as one-stop shops. And this is where you — the reader of this book — will have the edge. For you will avoid being a one-stop shop. You will escape the mire of a desultory listing in your local Yellow Pages.

PERRi Entertainment Services Inc. refuses to be a one-stop shop. Small printing jobs are not us. We're large. We're specialists. We're kings in our field. We'd rather be in the Yearbook of Experts, Authorities & Spokespersons.

AFTER MUCH REVIEW AND analysis, I have come up with this list: the **Top 20 Fields Calling for Experts From Out of Town**. I assembled the list by perusing Fortune magazine's Fortune 500 list, entrepreneurial magazines, and trusting my own instincts. The list is not a be-all end-all of fine possibilities. If you have an idea to merge your passion with profession and it is not listed below, please don't allow its absence to deter you.

On the other hand, let me issue this warning: plenty of home-business and other entrepreneurial magazines are filled with advertisements and articles about flavor-of-the-month "cutting-edge" franchises to get into. My advice: steer clear of all these "hot" ideas. I am talking about gum ball machines, pay phones, car painting, mailbox companies, cracked windshield repair, and gold-by-the-inch sold in malls.

They are gimmicks. Stay away from any ad decorated with dollar bills or bags of money, tempting those who would get rich quick without breaking a sweat. Likewise, I hope you'll remain as cynical as I am whenever a half-hour paid advertisement appears on your television, full of giddy testimonies from folk who bought the advertiser's video and book and babble about being on their way to earning their first million. P.T. Barnum's famous quote about "suckers" need not be repeated here.

Remember, you have to be focused and specific in order to succeed as the expert from out of town. You cannot be merely a printer: you must be specialized, such as a printer for the international entertainment touring industry. You must not be a contractor; you must be specialized: such as a constructor of jails.

Nearly every Fortune 500 company began with an earnest soul or souls who focused on a specialty, and built from there. Maybe all they did was "build a better mouse trap." What they did not do was just build anything that customers asked them, whether it be a mouse trap, bear trap, or widget.

Top 20 Fields:

20) **Water misters.** Chicago and Las Vegas and other burgs that suffer from heat waves need these giant misters to cool the air outside large buildings. These contraptions have become more economical and feasible and are beginning to pop up all over.

19) **Printing.** The technology growth has truly slowed after the break-neck pace of the late 1980s and early '90s. Specialize in one industry, such as printing menus.

18, 17) **Bookkeeping/accounting.** You can be a specialty bookkeeper or accountant at just about anything.

16) **Computer system supplier/trainer.** Focus on a specific industry. Maybe you'll sell to restaurants only, or furniture stores.

15) **Construction.** I have a cousin who builds custom miniature golf courses. It is all he does. Find your niche.

14) **Graphic design.** Not to be confused with printing. Do not be a one-stop shop. If you happen to know, say, a lot about clothing, you might specialize in designing the merchandise, advertising and graphics for the clothing industry. Someone has to design the little tags that go on the backs of new jeans.

13) **Collection agency.** Again, do not be a one-stop shop. Focus on a specific industry. If a collection agency came along that catered to the entertainment touring business, it would make a mint.

12) **Home security.** Specialize in a certain clientele, such as entertainers.

11) **Travel agency.** A giant industry that could use more specialists.

10) **Multi-media.** A huge industry growing like mad. A need exists for specialists who can make compact discs incorporating sound and pictures for home computers.

Again, focus on a specific clientele, such as church groups.

9) **Electric Vehicles.** I promise you that EV's loom large on the horizon. You can specialize in anything from servicing parts for these cars of the future to being the person who installs EV battery re-chargers at traditional gasoline stations.

8) **Office environments.** Companies need consultants to make their work places ergonomically safer, and more environmentally "green" using earth-friendly materials and proper recycling.

7) **Safety books.** Every large employer must supply its own safety manual. Become an expert manual-writer for a specific industry, such as supermarkets.

6) **Wireless Communications.** This is a major industry, with its mobile radio and cellular phones. An expert at any aspect of this field, from repair to supplying offices to hooking up antennae, cannot miss.

5) **Home improvement remodeling services.** Be a specialist in one remodeling profession, such as installing Roman bath tubs. Customers will always invest in their homes.

4) **Insurance.** There are experts in insurance in all areas. PERRi actually has an agent that insures only our computer equipment. Find your niche and exploit it.

3) **TeleCommuting**. "The California in-home office thing" This is my own phrase. Legislation in the Golden State calls for having corporations in the near-future maintain a certain percentage of their employees working at home at their computers. A specialist in setting up and monitoring these home work stations will be in great demand.

2) **Recreation.** More and more, you will find theme parks, motion simulator theaters, virtual reality games, water parks and so on cropping up as the population grows and a baby boomlet continues to materialize. American leisure activity has clearly moved beyond bowling and tennis.

1) **The Internet.** This is going to be the medium of the 21st Century. We have television, radio and print. The media will now include the Internet. More people are signing on every day. The Internet is expanding at a rapid pace. You can become the expert consultant on creating websites on the Internet for specific industries. For example, the book-publishing industry. There will be so

many sub-divisions on the Internet, you will be able to become a "webmaster" for individual fields. You could, for example, specialize in creating Internet menus and home-delivery services for restaurants. Cyberspace is the new frontier.

In sum: don't think small, don't think "Yellow Pages." Think, <u>Yearbook of Experts, Authorities & Spokespersons</u>. That's where you belong. Think big. Think smart. Specialize and niche.

CONCLUSION

You have spent a lot of time now reading this book. Doubtless, your mind is filled with gorgeous visions of becoming a great success in business, by going where few in your field have gone before. I commend your discipline and congratulate you on your plans. You will soon experience the new energy of having customers in a nationwide market regard you with great respect, merely because you now have the mystique of the out-of-town expert working for you.

Here at the conclusion, you must remember — first and foremost — to not be afraid to take the next step in becoming the expert from out of town. What you must do now is avoid the trap of committing this book to a dusty shelf, or discarding it into storage oblivion to end up as garage sale fodder.

This book has served as a heady motivational tool. Now it must become a handy reference tool. Highlight the how-to chapter: Chapter Six with its networking tips, Chapter Seven with information on building a façade, Chapter Nine with its billing and bookkeeping advice. Other chapters, as you see fit. Know that it is human nature to freeze from taking action out of fear of the unknown. Don't fight this feeling. Just realize it for what it is, and move ahead. Remember that even mighty figures from Jesus to Leonardo to the present day have suffered and struggled under the weight of their home-town baggage. Yet they boldly struck out to reach broader audiences. The rest, as they say, is history.

You, too, must fly the nest.

JUST THE OTHER DAY I was in a bookstore. A particular title caught my eye: The Magic of Thinking Big. Its cover heralded a truly fantastic feat: "Acquire the secrets of success. Achieve everything you've always wanted." I winced. Friends, there is no book that will allow you to achieve everything you've always wanted. The book you are holding in your hands at this moment makes no such carnival barker-like boasts.

Now that you have finished its 12 chapters, you are fully one step closer to making yourself achieve what you've always wanted in business: becoming a prosperous entrepreneur. This book is not going to do this for you. *You* are going to do this for you. This book is not going to jump off the table and make your phone calls for you. Now that you've read, The Expert From Out of Town, use it as a guide, and seek out other business books oriented to your profession and situation. I have included in the back a reference guide of books that have helped me. Some are business books, others, motivational books.

Your next step after reading, The Expert From Out of Town may very well be developing your capacity for positive thinking. One of the titles I've recommended is, What to Say When You Talk to Yourself. How many people, after reading a self-help or marketing book or attending a pricey, all-day motivational seminar, get all hyped up, then return from the world of words and ideas to the everyday world, forgetting about the whole idea? It's understandable. The high of the moment burns off. What to Say When You Talk to Yourself is the only book I've read that touches on this very thing. There are also other valuable motivational books that will help you carry yourself forward, if you need such help.

NOW IS ALSO THE time, if you haven't done so already, to complete the equation of **KNOWLEDGE + PASSION = THE BUSINESS FOR YOU TO MASTER**. Keep your day job, but start exploring what special professional skills you have gained. Recognize your hobbies, your talents, your God-given gifts. Then push for the mental break-through by which you couple your skills and loves to yield the perfect specialized field for you.

Ultimately, you must use the M.E.S.H. theory. Master a trade. Expand your market. Sharpen in on a niche. Then get out there and hype. Let the world know you're the specialist in your area of expertise. You've got to begin today to start finding the "M" of the theory. Remember: you are the only one who can do anything for yourself. You're on your own, folks. Just know that the techniques described in this book worked for me. Let them work for you. Please indulge me by allowing me to share this quote I love from Theodore Roosevelt:

"It is not the critic who counts, not the man who points out how the strong man stumbled, or where the doer of deeds could have done better. The credit belongs to the man who is actually in the arena; whose face is marred by dust and sweat and blood; who strives valiantly; who errs and comes short again and again; who knows the great enthusiasms, the great devotions, and spends himself in a worthy cause; who, at the best, knows in the end the triumph of high achievement; and who, at the worst, if he fails, at least while daring greatly, so that his place shall never be with those cold and timid souls who know neither VICTORY nor DEFEAT."

You will never know whether you've found a niche or specialty business that will allow you to become an expert from out of town, unless you go out now and try. The great hockey player Wayne Gretzky said, "You miss 100 percent of the shots you never take." But if you continue to push ahead, even if you stumble or fail several times, I believe that the odds are great that you'll ultimately reach your goal. When you do, when you become the expert from out of town, write me a letter. I just may include your story in this book's sequel.

RECOMMENDED READING

The Abuse Excuse, by Alan M. Dershowitz. Little, Brown and Co. ISBN: 0-316-18135-8. Being a fan of accounting for one's own behavior, I find this to be one of the greatest books of the 1990s. In a time when a person can sue a shopping mall after slipping on ice while wearing high heels, this book should have a place in the Required Reading Hall of Fame.

The Bible. Read this and you will realize why it has been around for a very long time. Inspiring stories; great pieces of wisdom.

How to Protect Your Business, by the Council of Better Business Bureaus, Prentice Hall. ISBN: 0-87502-143-3. Many business people have recommended this to me over the years. A primer on handling everything from bankruptcy fraud to cargo theft to office supply schemes.

The Quick and Easy Way to Effective Speaking, by Dale Carnegie. Dale Carnegie & Associates, Inc. As an expert from out of town, you are bound to find yourself at some point speaking in public, so what better person to learn from than the guy who practically invented the science? Though some of this great man's ideals have gone out of style, getting up and speaking is still as scary as it was when he wrote his book.

Starting Your Own Business, by Stephen C. Harper. McGraw-Hill. ISBN: 0-07-026685-9. This book gets down to the nitty-gritty of starting a business.

The Tao of Pooh, by Benjamin Hoff. Penguin Books. ISBN: 0-14-0067-47-7. What can I say? I love this book. It teaches how to stay happy and calm under all circumstances. It also teaches in a wonderful way about taking responsibility for your actions.

What to Say When You Talk to Yourself, by Shad Helmstetter. Pocket Books. ISBN: 0-671-70882-1. The best book on positive thinking that I have ever read.

Emotional Intelligence, by Daniel Goleman. Bantam. ISBN: 0-553-09503-X. Some call Emotional Intelligence the pop-psychology book of the nineties. This book will no-doubt earn its way into the classroom. An absolutely wonderful look at emotions and the social aspects of human nature.

The Popcorn Report, by Faith Popcorn. Harper Business. ISBN: 0-88730-594-6. No Expert is complete without a marketing strategy, and this book by Faith Popcorn will help you get on track by looking at trends. From Cocooning to Cashing Out, Faith looks at the direction of the future.

Guerrilla Marketing, by Jay Conrad Levinson. Houghton Mikklin. ISBN: 0-395-64496-8. You have heard about it, I had heard about it, but until I read it, I believed it. This is a great book for small businesses.

Pick a better Country, by Ken Hamblin. Simon & Schuster. ISBN: 0-684-80755-6. Mr. Hamblin throws out a challenge "Pick a better Country". It will inspire every citizen to reinvest in the American Dream.

Practical Intuition, by Laura Day. Villard. ISBN: 0-679-44932-9. You know when the phone rings, and you know who's calling -- that is your intuition working. Laura shows you how to harness this power and make it work for you.